Journal of Beat Studies

Volume 4, 2016

PACE UNIVERSITY PRESS • NEW YORK

Copyright © 2016 by
Pace University Press
41 Park Row, 15th Floor
New York, NY 10038

All rights reserved
Printed in the United States of America

ISSN 2165-8706
ISBN: 978-0-9619518-4-9 (pbk: alk.ppr.)

Member

Council of Editors of Learned Journals

♾ Paper used in this publication meets the minimum requirements of
American National Standard for Information
Sciences–Permanence of Paper for Printed Library Materials,
ANSI Z39.48–1984

Editors

Ronna C. Johnson	Tufts University
Nancy M. Grace	The College of Wooster

Editorial Board

Ann Charters	University of Connecticut—Storrs (emerita)
Maria Damon	Pratt Institute of Art
Terence Diggory	Skidmore College (emeritus)
Tim Gray	CUNY Staten Island
Oliver Harris	Keele University, United Kingdom
Allen Hibbard	Middle Tennessee State University
Tim Hunt	Illinois State University
Cary Nelson	University of Illinois
A. Robert Lee	The University of Murcia, Spain
Jennie Skerl	West Chester University (retired)
David Sterritt	Long Island University (emeritus)
Tony Trigilio	Columbia College—Chicago
John Tytell	CUNY Queens College
John Whalen-Bridge	National University of Singapore, Singapore

Production Staff

Stephanie Hsu	Production Editor, Pace University
Mary Katherine Cornfield	Graduate Assistant, Pace University Press
Angela Taldone	Graduate Assistant, Pace University Press

Journal of Beat Studies

Volume 4, 2016

	vi	Letter from the Editors
Micheal Sean Bolton	1	William S. Burroughs, Michel Serres, and the Word Parasite
Jane Falk	17	The Beats and Independent Film: A Different Cast of Characters
Anne Lovering Rounds	35	Allen Ginsberg's Ambivalent Whitman
John Whalen-Bridge	43	Gary Snyder, Counterculture, and National Identity

THE BEAT INTERVIEW

Amy Friedman	57	Rochelle Owens

REVIEWS

Todd Giles	75	*Crowded by Beauty: The Life and Zen of Poet Philip Whalen* by David Schneider

Maria Damon	81	*Elise Cowen: Poems and Fragments* by Elise Cowen, edited by Tony Trigilio
Michael J. Dittman	88	*Conversations with Ken Kesey* edited by Scott F. Parker
Jack Ryan	92	*The Village: 400 Years of Beats and Bohemians, Radicals and Rogues, a History of Greenwich Village* by John Strausbaugh
Jennie Skerl	100	*Call Me Burroughs: A Life* by Barry Miles
Katharine Streip	108	*The Soft Machine: The Restored Text* by William S. Burroughs, edited and with an introduction by Oliver Harris; *The Ticket That Exploded: The Restored Text* by William S. Burroughs, edited and with an introduction by Oliver Harris; *Nova Express: The Restored Text* by William S. Burroughs, edited and with an introduction by Oliver Harris
	113	The Beat Index
	150	Call for Submissions for Volume 5
	151	Call for Essay Proposals for MLA Volume
	152	Essay Abstracts
	154	Notes on Contributors
	157	Editorial Policy

Letter from the Editors

Ten years ago, the Beat Studies Association (BSA) was formed, and five years ago, the BSA entered into a relationship with Pace University Press to publish the first-ever scholarly journal devoted to Beat Generation writers and art. It is with gratitude that we have continued this important scholarly work and are proud to introduce the fourth volume of the *Journal of Beat Studies*. This volume contains essays on Gary Snyder, William S. Burroughs, Allen Ginsberg, Diane di Prima, ruth weiss, Helen Adam, and Joanne Kyger, along with reviews of scholarly works on Ken Kesey, Elise Cowen, Philip Whalen, Burroughs, and Greenwich Village. Of particular interest is our new Beat Studies Interview, which will become a regular feature in each volume. Our inaugural interview with playwright Rochelle Owens was conducted by Amy Friedman, a long-time Beat scholar and a member of the BSA editorial board. As was the case with volume three, we have continued the Beat Index, a compendium of current Beat scholarship nationally and internationally. The Index wouldn't exist without the work of Harrison Todd and Nan Denette, English majors from The College of Wooster, who serve as our research assistants. As readers can see by simply perusing the Index compiled by Harrison and Nan, scholarly interests in the Beats is alive and well.

We also hope that readers like the new look of the *Journal*. It wasn't a major make-over, but the *JBS* now has a cleaner more vibrant appearance thanks to Manuela Soares and her production team of Pace publishing graduate students, Mary Katherine Cornfield and Angela Taldone. We especially thank Stephanie Hsu, assistant professor of English at Pace, for her excellent copy editing of this volume. Her attention to detail and capacious approach to developing a formal *JBS* style guide have already gone a long way toward strengthening the quality of the journal. We look forward to a long and collegial relationship with everyone on the team.

The fifth volume of the *Journal* will include a series of essays in honor of Ann Charters, the first president of the BSA and in many respects the founder of the field of Beat Studies. We have included a Call for Essays on Charters, posted at the end of the volume. Writers interested in contributing to this collection should contact us as soon as possible with their essay ideas or submissions.

Onward!
Ronna C. Johnson and Nancy M. Grace

William S. Burroughs, Michel Serres, and the Word Parasite
Micheal Sean Bolton

The bit of noise, the small random element, transforms one system or one order into another. To reduce this otherness to contradiction is to reduce everything to violence and war. —Michel Serres

Much critical work has been devoted to William S. Burroughs's characterization of language as a parasitic entity, a word virus, which infiltrates, feeds upon, and otherwise victimizes its human hosts. The word virus and its many derivations—e.g., the Other Half, Genial, the Death Dwarves—provide a recurring motif throughout four of Burroughs's early novels: *Naked Lunch* (1959), *The Soft Machine* (1961, 1966), *The Ticket that Exploded* (1962, 1967), and *Nova Express* (1964). Critical consensus maintains that the word virus functions as a mechanism for the oppression of human subjects, and is usually employed by malevolent, often alien, bureaucratic organizations such as the operators of the Trak Reservation, the Garden of Delights, and the Ovens of Minraud, all of which might be subdivisions of the Nova Mob. Robin Lydenberg, for example, explains, "Beneath the specific abuses of politics, science, or personal relations, Burroughs traces this cutting edge of domination and control to its insidious origin in language" (30). And Jennie Skerl notes, "The Word virus controls our concept of reality and imposes a dualism that makes it impossible to change reality" (60). Although these critics often recognize that Burroughs employs experimental techniques to subvert the control mechanisms of the word virus by, as Allen Hibbard writes, "putting words together in new combinations and disseminating them as a sort of inoculation or counter-virus" (15), they do not address the potential for using parasitic language to effect positive change in the human host. In order to see beyond the destructive qualities of the word virus, different conceptions of parasitism as well as subjectivity must be applied. Posthuman theory offers concepts necessary to understanding the transformative potential of the word virus. The work of Michel Serres is particularly useful for reassessing the parasitic functions of the word virus.

Posthuman theory, as I have written elsewhere, investigates the question of "what remains or arises after the dissolution of the liberal humanist subject" (14). The posthuman subject abandons liberal humanism's autonomy and agency for multiplicity, fluidity, and interconnection, which are qualities notably found in Burroughs's characters. From its beginnings, posthumanism has been aligned with second order systems theory and, thus, "sees the human as embedded within an environment, an instantiation of a series of information exchanges, transfers of data and feedback mechanisms" (Nayar 35). The human subject, in other words, is regarded as an interdependent, and indeed co-evolving, system among other systems, including communication systems such as language.

Recently, Cary Wolfe has offered a reassessment of Serres's philosophical work *The Parasite* (1980) as a seminal work of posthuman theory. Wolfe's introduction, "Bring the Noise: *The Parasite* and the Multiple Genealogies of Posthumanism," focuses attention on the parasite's role as noise that interrupts the flow of information through a system and, subsequently, allows for the autopoiesis, or self-reorganization of the system. As Wolfe explains, "[N]oise, the event, constantly forces temporarily homeostatic systems of interaction to reconstitute and reorganize themselves" (xv). The parasite's disruptions, then, do not simply subvert or oppose the structure of the system, but also constitute a necessary event in a process of reconfiguration and renewal of the system. Viewed as posthuman theory, *The Parasite* offers a lens through which Burroughs's parasitical language virus may also be seen as a positive, even revolutionary, agent in Burroughs's project, which aims not only to subvert the control structures of language, but also to effect changes in human subjects through language. Burroughs's various strategies for the randomization of language provide the parasitic noise that serves to disrupt and to reconfigure language systems and, subsequently, the human subjects that are parasited by language.

The application of Serres's theories is not new to Burroughs criticism. In her study of Burroughs's experimental novels, *Word Cultures: Radical Theory and Practice in William S. Burroughs' Fiction* (1987), Lydenberg devotes a chapter to the concept of the parasite as it appears in Burroughs's work. The chapter opens with a short description of Serres's *The Parasite* and notes similarities between his host/parasite binary and the binary of the human individual and institutional bureaucracies in Burroughs's novels. The comparison is very compelling, but sadly after about two pages, she moves on to discussions of other theorists, particularly Roland Barthes and J. Hillis Miller. Of course, Lydenberg has good reasons for this decision, not the least of which is that a sustained exploration of the correspondences between Serres and Burroughs would diverge from her central thesis regarding Burroughs's privileging of a heightened literalness in his language as opposed to metaphor and abstraction. Serres's ideas certainly tend toward abstraction, and Lydenberg is more interested in the concrete effects of parasitism on the body of the host than in metaphors of mice or systems theory. There is also a clear advantage for her in considering the notion of the parasite from more than one theoretical perspective, as Barthes and Miller both offer important perspectives on the relationship between language and parasitism. Still, the brevity of Lydenberg's discussion leaves readers to wonder what a more sustained examination of Serres's ideas might offer to readings of Burroughs.

Lydenberg recognizes that for Serres, at least, "the parasite is the archetype of all relations of power; but it is also the agent of change which disrupts those relations" (127). However, her focus on the destructive qualities of the parasite prevents her from exploring the operation of parasitical noise as a positive force, "an agent of change," in Burroughs's novels. Though she notes the complexity and non-duality of the parasite as presented in Serres's book, her application of his notion of the parasite to Burroughs's texts explores only the destructive aspect of parasitism, as parasitic bureaucracies are locked into a relationship of conflict with human characters. She observes that "Burroughs denounces as parasitic all systems of social control" (128); subsequently, she focuses her discussion on the destructive nature of the word virus as "[t]he parasitic power of bureaucracy...based on the control of information and the power of speech, particularly that imperial speech which silences all other speakers" (127). Here Lydenberg not only stays true to her thesis, but she is clearly following Serres's point when he writes "Who has the power? The one who has the sound, the noise, and who makes others be quiet.... To say anything at all, but to prevent others from saying" (*Parasite* 142). This strategy of silencing others is rendered literally in the actions of the Sender faction of *Naked Lunch*. Burroughs explains that a Sender can only ever send: "[h]e can never receive, because if he receives that means someone else has feelings of his own could louse up his continuity" (*Naked* 137). The Sender can never acknowledge the subjecthood of the other, and so, there must never be two-way communication between Sender and receiver. Such an exchange would risk empathy and a reversal of roles. Thus, the key to the Sender's control strategy is always and only to transmit information, never to receive it. In this way, the Sender controls the flow of information and occupies the top position of "the economics of exchange which Burroughs detects behind all human relations" (Lydenberg 128). Lydenberg explains that such "hierarchical structure[s] of domination and control" represent "bureaucracy in the form of a pyramid of cannibalism," with those at the top of the pyramid feeding on those below (128, 129).

Steven D. Brown and Paul Stenner note a similar configuration in what they call Serres's "parasitical cascade": a one-way relationship in which more complex systems feed off of lower order systems by a process of parasitic repetition. They describe the cascade as "a kind of chain of parasites, which forms a clear sequence where each position in turn successfully parasites the former" (47). Then they admit that "this is not so much a chain as a cascade, where the produce flows down through the chain of parasites" and "[e]ach link is formed by a one-way relationship of taking without giving" (47). In Serres's words, "The system constructed here beginning with a production...is parasitic in a cascade" in which a given production "is always immediately parasited," i.e., repeated or reproduced for the profit of the parasite (5, 4). He describes the "bureaucratic" power holder as the entity at the top of the cascade: "The producer plays the contents, the parasite, the position. The one who plays the position will always beat the one who plays the contents. The latter is simple and naïve; the former is complex and mediatized. The parasite always beats the producer" (38). The parasite in this case is the bureaucracy that feeds on the work of the producer and offers nothing in exchange. Burroughs characterizes these power holders as "the welchers, kid, who can't cover their bets and never intended to cover...all the 'Mr Martins' who are trying to buy something for nothing" (*Ticket* 137). Eventually, the parasitic bureaucracy will exhaust the host-producer and the system will collapse like "a virus that has killed the host" (*Naked* 113). In order to survive, then, the bureaucracy must continually find new producers to exploit and exhaust.

The destructive potential of the parasite in Burroughs's novels corresponds to what Wolfe characterizes as the biological aspect of parasitism in Serres's theory, which posits that parasite/host relationships can move in only one direction (xiii). Serres regards "biological" parasitic relationships as "one-way relations, where one eats the other and where the second cannot benefit at all from the first" (5). An episode in *Ticket* similarly represents a case of one-way, destructive parasitism as "a *biologic* weapon that reduces healthy clean-minded men to abject slobbering inhuman things undoubtedly of virus origins" (*Ticket* 5, emphasis mine). Though the destructive aspect of the parasite often appears in the form of a biologic virus—e.g., Virus B-23 in the later novel, *Cities of the Red Night*—the word virus also reflects this characteristic of Serres's parasite.

Burroughs critics surely have something very much like Serres's "biological" sense of parasitism in mind when they characterize the word virus as "language which appropriates life and gives nothing in return" (Lydenberg 127). In *Nova Express*, Burroughs describes the parasite as virus in very similar terms:

> What does virus do wherever it can dissolve a hole and find traction?—It starts eating—And what does it do with what it eats?—It makes exact copies of itself that start eating to make more copies that start eating and so forth to the virus power the fear hate virus slowly replaces the host with virus copies. (73)

In a routine satirizing capitalist imperialism, the character of Clem declares, "We have come to feed on your backwardness" (*Naked* 119). When the Nationalist complains, "Don't you realize my people are hungry?" Clem replies, "That's the way I like to see them" (*Naked* 119). As with Serres's bureaucrats, only the parasitic power holders feed. The colonized starve even as they are fed upon, metaphorically if not literally.

BURROUGHS, SERRES, AND THE WORD PARASITE *Bolton*

Often in the novels, Burroughs depicts the word virus or parasite as non-biological code. For example, *The Soft Machine* features Mayan codices, which the bureaucratic priestly caste use for "one-way telepathic broadcasts instructing the workers what to feel and when" (*Naked* 137). The narrator of "The Mayan Caper" experiences these broadcasts as "the crushing weight of evil insect control forcing my thoughts and feelings into prearranged molds, squeezing my spirit in a soft invisible vise" (*Soft* 89). Here the parasitism is ideological rather than biological, but again the power holders thrive by feeding on the producers in the society while the producers languish. The frequency in the novels of such one-way relationships lends legitimacy to critics' focus on the destructive aspects of the word parasite.

However, the relationship between the host and parasite is neither so stable nor so easily defined as discussions of Burroughs's use of the idea seem to suggest. Nick Redfern notes that, for Serres, the relationship exhibits another way in which "[t]he binary opposition of host/parasite dissolves into indeterminacy, and the parasitic control of bureaucracy is founded upon the control of the information that allows us to define our position in relation to the medium" (10). The roles of the host and parasite are therefore interchangeable and, at times, not easy to distinguish. Though moving in only one direction, the relationship eventually feeds back upon itself with both host and parasite feeding off of the function of the other. Serres characterizes this aspect of the host/parasite exchange as an "intersubjective relationship" in which "[the parasite] obtains energy and pays for it in information" (8, 36). The host, then, feeds on the information offered by the parasite, blurring the distinction between the two. This "intersubjective relationship" is one of social exchange in which, unlike the "biological" relationship, both parties benefit to some degree from the interaction, though one may still exploit the other. Ultimately, as Lydenberg herself notes, "[t]he binary opposition of parasite/host thus dissolves into indeterminacy" (127).

Indeterminacy is, in fact, a key feature of Burroughs's characters as they constantly shift and exchange names, identities, and even bodies. His exemplar of indeterminacy is the character of Mr Bradley Mr Martin who appears throughout the Nova Trilogy (comprised of *The Soft Machine, The Ticket That Exploded,* and *Nova Express*) and is described as a "five times guided poisonous cloud of parasites" (*Ticket* 173). Mr Bradley Mr Martin appears as both a single entity (as seen in my first quotation from *Ticket*) and as two separate characters whose identities seem to be interchangeable. For example, Burroughs offers this description of the character/s in a passage from *Nova Express*: "Martin fished in the evening with Bradley who slept in the bunk next to his or in his bunk back and forth changing bodies in the blue silence—Tasks shifted with poker play and flesh trade" (125-26). The "flesh trade" can be taken both figuratively and literally, as a sexual exchange or as actual body swapping. Even when Bradley and Martin are rendered as seemingly separate beings, their discrete identities are unstable and interchangeable in a way similar to Serres's host and parasite.

Timothy Murphy further suggests that Mr Bradley Mr Martin "may also be an autoparasitic double star that consumes itself" (126). Here Murphy references Mr Bradley Mr Martin's appearance as a symbiotic star pairing in which Mr Bradley is "a small hot blue star" and Mr Martin is "a larger red star" from which "the blue star constantly pulls fuel in the form of hydrogen gas" (*Nova* 74). This parasitic relationship will inevitably result in the death of both stars as the re-fueled, blue star explodes. This apocalyptic outcome is reflected in his/their more significant role as leader of the Nova Mob. In this role, Mr Bradley Mr Martin works to bring about the destruction of the host planet that he/they and the Mob occupy through the introduction of binary conflicts. Upon the destruction of a planet, they move on to the next planet and begin the process again. However, like the parasite, Mr Bradley Mr Martin will eventually run out of hosts and bring about his/their own destruction.

The autoparasitic and self-destructive behaviors of Mr Bradley Mr Martin parallel those of Burroughs's language virus in the form of the "Other Half." The "Other Half" is, after all, "'You' next time around—born when you die" (*Ticket* 160). But as Burroughs states elsewhere, a parasite "can exhibit living qualities only in a host, by using the life of another" (*Naked* 113). For the "Other Half" to live beyond its birth at the death of its host, it must shift roles and become both parasite and host. It must, in a true sense, become "you next time around," a host already infected by itself as word parasite. Serres similarly maintains, "Men parasite men, man is a host to man...The relation parasites the relation; the relation itself is a parasite" (*Parasite* 132). Steven Shaviro elucidates this point, observing that, for Burroughs, "Self-identity is ultimately a symptom of parasitic invasion, the expression within me of forces originating from outside" (102). For Burroughs as well as Serres, the intersubjectivity and interdependence of the host and parasite result in the dissolution of the binary, as the pair constantly switch roles and confuse identities. As Serres explains, "The parasited one parasites the parasites" (13).

Further complicating the interdependence of host and parasite, Serres claims, "The difference is part of the thing itself, and perhaps even produces the thing. Maybe the radical origin of things is really that difference" (13). Lydenberg similarly notes that "[o]ne is never without the parasite for the parasite is the embodiment of difference and therefore the source of all identity, of all change, of life itself" (128). Not only can the host define itself through its differential relation to the parasite, but this differential relation offers the possibility for change and growth. And Burroughs makes a similar assertion through the character of The Rube: "I am not two—I am *one*—But to maintain my state of oneness I need twoness in other life forms—Other must talk so that I can remain silent" (*Nova* 77). These statements point to what is perhaps the most intriguing aspect of the parasite, especially in regard to Burroughs's works: its role as the disruptive noise that triggers the reorganization of the system.

Genesis (1982), Serres's follow-up book to *The Parasite*, conducts an extended meditation on the productive aspects of noise. Serres proposes that noise and its chaos are the very foundations from which meaning and order arise. He asserts, "Noise is the basic element of the software of all our logic, or it is to the logos what matter used to be to form. Noise is the background information, the material of that form" (*Genesis* 7). It is from the raw material of noise that meaning and logic are constructed. Noise is intrinsic in meaning; it "is a turbulence, it is order and disorder at the same time, order revolving on itself through repetition and redundancy, disorder through chance occurrences" (*Genesis* 59). As such, "[n]oise has no contradictory" (*Genesis* 61), and thus has the potential to disrupt the binaries from which meaning and order are typically constructed. Noise is both the raw material from which a system is constructed and the necessary factor for the system's disruption and reorganization.

The Nova Trilogy features resistance forces as "*non-organization* the aim of which is to immunize our agents against fear despair and death. . .to break the birth-death cycle" (*Ticket* 10). For Burroughs, the "birth-death cycle" is a product of virus replication that the disorder of the resistance serves to disrupt. The figurehead of disorder and disruption as presented in Ticket is Pan, the god of panic: "God of Panic piping blue notes—invisible intervention—last round over—last parasite muttering there: 'Man, like good bye then'" (82). Like Serres's noise, the disharmony of Pan's blue notes is a turbulence that provides the disruptive force, the "invisible intervention," to break the replication process of the parasitical virus.

In its disruptive function, Serres's noise perhaps most resembles Burroughs's mythologized apomorphine anti-virus. Like Serres's noise, apomorphine nullifies restrictive meaning and order, as "[a]pomorphine is no word and no image" (*Nova* 48). Especially in *Nova Express*, apomorphine represents a strategy for combating the parasitic word virus. The character, or simulated character, of Mr. Winkhorst proposes: "Apomorphine combats virus invasion by simulating the regulatory centers to normalize metabolism—A powerful variation of this drug could deactivate all verbal units and blanket the earth in silence" (*Nova* 39). The notion of "blanket[ing] the earth in silence" suggests that this silence is loaded. Rather than a total absence of sound, nothingness, there seems to be an absence of meaningful language akin to the turbulence of Serres's noise. Apomorphine induces this condition by interrupting the replication process of the word virus and "disintegrat[ing] verbal units" in order to avert the inevitable outcome of the virus' proliferation: nova explosion (*Nova* 40). The disruptive functions of apomorphine and of noise can thus be used to produce liberating effects: "Good bye parasite invasion with weakness of dual structure, as the shot of apomorphine exploded mold of their claws in vomit" (*Ticket* 106). Apomorphine reduces the ordered mold of parasite claws to the formless disorder of vomit.

Wolfe's introduction to the 2007 edition of *The Parasite* draws attention to and places emphasis on the positive role of the parasite as noise, remarking that "noise is *productive* and creative" (xiii). The effects of noise are integral to the production of new systems. "Mistakes, wavy lines, confusion, obscurity are part of knowledge," according to Serres, "noise is part of communication" (*Parasite* 12). For example, the Senders, described in *Naked Lunch* as "the Human Virus" (141), are opposed by the Factualists who intervene in the Senders' propagandist messages with facts, thus interrupting the messages by using information as noise (136). In much the same way that apomorphine operates as noise that breaks the cycle of virus replication, Factualist information distorts the Senders' message and disrupts the proliferation of their propaganda. As Serres tells us, "The host counter-parasites his guests, not by taking away his food from them (first meaning) but by making noise (second meaning)" (*Parasite* 52). The Factualists, then, oppose the parasitical behavior of the Senders not by obliterating the message but by interrupting it, by acting as parasites themselves, though in a positive rather than destructive sense.

Of course, the most frequent and striking occurrences of parasitical noise in Burroughs's novels arise from his application of randomizing techniques in his narratives, most particularly the cut-up and fold-in techniques of the Nova Trilogy. These techniques are often viewed by critics as subversive attempts to destroy the control mechanisms of language, with no productive outcomes other than opening the possibility of liberation from those control mechanisms. Lydenberg writes that though his narrative experimentation seeks "to make accessible to [readers] the liberating effects of his techniques for the manipulation of language. . . Burroughs' purpose is not to incite reform" (xi 9). And Katherine Hayles argues that, though his randomizing strategy "aims to break the reader not only out of personal obsessions but also out of the surrounding, culturally constructed envelope of sounds and words . . . the emphasis remains on subversion and disruption rather than creative rearticulation" (213, 220). These views recognize the value of disrupting systems of control but fail to find any constructive effects—either for social and individual reform or for narrative reinvention—produced by random narratives.

The interpretation of Burroughs's randomizing factors as methods of disruption and subversion corresponds to Serres's discussion of harmony and noise. For Serres, harmony and order lead to stasis, to a sort of death. He proposes: "As far as I know, perfect tuning is not the height of art, and perhaps it is only its misery. Might harmony be a somewhat excited variety of flatness? Might it be an antechamber of death?" (*Parasite* 126). Serres's characterization of harmony as stasis is reflected in Burroughs's notion of the "orgasm death tune" (*Ticket* 111), a feedback loop that locks subjects into the never-ending cycle of birth and death.

BURROUGHS, SERRES, AND THE WORD PARASITE Bolton

And the cycle of birth and death is, as previously observed, akin to viral replication.

In terms of the word virus, Arndt Niebisch explains, "Burroughs establishes the idea of a negative feedback, in which the virus creates over generations a stable symbiosis with its host, i.e., eliminates noise" (5). As noted above, Burroughs proposes the use of apomorphine as a disruptive agent to break "the circuit of positive feedback" of the orgasm death tune (*Ticket* 111). Here he may be referring to the phenomenon of regenerative feedback, where the "the system's codifier is reversed so it responds to positive feedback with positive feedback," which can lead to "pathology and ultimately self-destruction" (Bales 37). This destruction results from amplifying noise in a system to the point of total chaos. But the application of apomorphine—itself a sort of noise—to disrupt the repetitive circuit of the orgasm death tune suggests that Burroughs more likely has negative feedback in mind.

Information theory provides a useful way in which to understand Burroughs's feedback metaphor and its relationship to his strategy of narrative randomization. It defines negative feedback as feedback used to dampen errors in a signal, to reduce, or as Niebisch suggests, to eliminate noise and difference—the difference that might be "the radical origin of things," in the words of Serres (*Parasite* 13). Earlier in *Ticket*, Burroughs himself characterizes positive feedback differently, writing "positive feedback Pan God of panic piping blue notes through empty streets as the berserk time machine twisted a tornado of centuries" (30). As noted earlier, Pan represents the disruptive, randomizing noise that breaks the process of virus replication that tends toward stasis. This characterization more closely reflects the function of positive feedback in information theory, as feedback that intensifies rather than dampens difference. The orgasm death tune, in contrast, exemplifies negative feedback's process of repetition toward order and stasis.

Burroughs's word virus most often functions in the manner of negative feedback, creating exact copies of itself in order to eradicate difference by "transform[ing] an individual into the 'Human Virus'" (Lydenberg 131). The outcome of this process is analogous to that of the Divisionist agenda to "cut off tiny bits of their flesh and grow exact replicas of themselves in embryo jelly . . . eventually there will be only one replica of one sex on the planet: that is one person in the world with millions of separate bodies" (*Naked* 137). The goal of producing noise through randomization is to disrupt this process of static repetition. Burroughs explains, "The only thing *not* prerecorded in a prerecorded universe is the prerecording itself which is to say *any* recording that contains a random factor" (*Ticket* 49). The random factor is disruptive parasitic noise, the dissonance and disorder that interrupts harmony and order.

Certainly, this interruption of oppressive order can be liberating in its destructive aspect; however, Serres's parasitical noise also performs a more productive function. For Serres, the disruptions created by parasitic noise force subjects to reorder themselves into new and more complex configurations. He writes, "The new order appears by the parasite troubling the message. It disconcerts the ancient series, order, and message; and then composes [*concerte*] new ones" (*Parasite* 184). The parasite therefore not only disrupts the old order, but also composes the new. Oliver Harris notes the same effect in Burroughs's randomization of language, in which "the sign creates its referent; production replaces reproduction" (178). Burroughs's randomization strategy, like Serres's parasite, operates not only as disruptive noise, but also as a necessary condition for producing change. As Allen Hibbard notes, "Rather than simply launching attacks on the existing structures, it allows alternative forms of organization based on libertarian principles to emerge" (18). Murphy advises that it is not until the Red Night Trilogy—*Cities of the Red Night* (1981), *The Place of Dead Roads* (1983), and *The Western Lands* (1987)—that Burroughs "offers affirmative ways to reorganize society in order to avoid the powerful dialectics of social and linguistic control" (5); however, such societal reorganization is prefigured by the reordering and reimagining of narrative that Burroughs accomplishes in the earlier experimental novels. In Burroughs's words, "[I]f you want to challenge and change fate. . . cut up the words. Make them make a new world" (*Conversations* 67). The goal of randomization in these novels is not simply disruption but the reconfiguration of language and, thus, of the human subjects that language parasites.

    Burroughs characterizes this operation of the parasite on the host subject as follows: "No matter how tight Security, I am always somewhere *Outside* giving orders and *Inside* this straightjacket of jelly that gives and stretches but always reforms ahead of every movement, thought, impulse" (*Naked* 185). As with Serres's, Burroughs's parasite operates on the subject from the outside and from the inside simultaneously to enact change. The parasite represents at once an alien outsider and the subject itself. By means of parasitic noise, the subject can disrupt its own homeostasis and reorder itself into new configurations. Examples of such transmutations of characters are ubiquitous in the novels, from Agent Lee's discorporation in *Nova Express*, or the gender and race switch of the narrator of "The Market" in *Naked Lunch*, to Clem Snide's transformation into Audrey Carsons in *Cities of the Red Night*, or Joe the Dead's shedding of his restrictive Kim Carsons persona in *Western Lands*.

    Burroughs exemplifies this conception of bodily transformation as a process of reformation and renewal in the following passage from *Soft Machine*, which offers a view of human evolutionary transmutation utilizing the cut-up technique:

> human faces tentative flicker in and out of focus. We waded into the warm mud-water. hair and ape flesh off in screaming strips. stood naked human bodies covered with phosphorescent green jelly. soft tentative flesh cut with ape

wounds. peeling other genitals. fingers and tongues rubbing off the jelly-cover. body melting pleasure-sounds in the warm mud. till the sun went and a blue wind of silence touched human faces and hair. When we came out of the mud we had names (174).

The evolution from ape to human in the passage is notably accompanied by the development of language through the acquisition of names. The cut-up later reveals that the transformation and its engendering of language—"sound thru our throats and swap we had names"—are accompanied by the presence of a "white worm-thing inside" (*Soft* 175). Though the parasitic worm-thing consumes some of the pre-human "hairy men," it also initiates the changes that allow others to survive: "Those lived who learned to let the softness in" (*Soft* 176). Like Serres's parasite, the worm-thing has the potential both for destruction and for positive transformation. The cut-up continues to trace the development of humans through to modern civilization: "Migrants of ape in gasoline crack of history, explosive bio-advance out of space to neon" (*Soft* 178). The parasite that consumes also triggers evolutionary change and human societal advancement.

Burroughs further expressed interest in the possibility of viral impact on human evolution in interviews. On at least two occasions, he discussed the related theories of viral evolution, which holds that "evolutionary change is biological mutation [over] one or two generations, possibly through a virus" (*Conversations* 153). And the "punctuational view of evolution, which says that if you take a species of fish from one place and put them in a completely foreign environment, they will mutate very rapidly. Alterations occur in response to drastic alterations in equilibrium in small, isolated groups" (*Conversations* 174). Burroughs admitted that "no virus we know of right now acts in this way" (*Conversations* 174); however, these theories seem to have influenced many of the transmutation scenes found throughout the novels.

Of course, the transformations in the novels are not always positive and are often horrific, but the potential for transformation provides a means for liberation—from the oppression of body, identity, gender, and any number of factors used for societal control—through the reconfiguration of the human subject into new and hybrid forms. According to Hayles, "Where hope exists in *Ticket*, it appears as posthuman mutations like the fish boy, whose fluidity perhaps prefigures a type of subjectivity attuned to the froth of noise" (220). Posthuman theory proposes that such reconfigurations result from introducing randomness into complex systems, such as narratives and human subjects. Hayles notes that "randomness has increasingly been seen to play a fruitful role in the evolution of complex systems" (286). Much like Serres's concept of noise, randomness is regarded here "not only as the lack of pattern but as the creative ground from which pattern can emerge" (*Parasite*

286). Just as noise "is order and disorder at the same time" for Serres (*Genesis* 59), "pattern and randomness are bound together in a complex dialectic that makes them not so much opposites as complements or supplements to one another," according to Hayles (25). Following this principle, the parasitic language of Burroughs's narratives not only disrupts and subverts conventional narrative meaning, but also provides the basic material from which an alternative narrative form is constructed.

Lydenberg explains that an important function of the cut-up method is "to make the writer's medium tangible—to make the word an object detached from its context, its author, its signifying function" (44). Indeed, the process of cutting up the text physically interrupts its order and meaning. But Hayles's posthuman perspective recognizes a more radical and productive outcome of the method:

> This technique hints that the technology [of the material text] is not merely a medium to represent thoughts that already exist but is itself capable of dynamic interactions *producing* the thoughts it describes. At issue, then, is the technology not as theme but as an articulation capable of producing new kinds of subjectivities. (216-17)

Richard Doyle echoes this point, asserting that Burroughs's "recombinant texts could be seen to be recipes for the alteration of consciousness" (240). And Burroughs himself insists upon the construction of the human subject through writing: "These colorless sheets are what flesh is made from—Becomes flesh when it has color and writing—That is Word and image write the message that is you on colorless sheets determine all flesh" (*Nova* 28). Rewriting "the message that is you" amounts to reconfiguring the subject into a new order. So, even as the word virus can bring about the destruction of the human host through static repetition, the cut-up method and other randomizing techniques can interrupt this repetition and induce the reconfiguration of the host by employing a different, productive aspect of parasitic language.

In the *Nova Express* chapter, "This Horrible Case," Burroughs demonstrates the process by folding a passage from Franz Kafka's *The Trial* (1925) into documents from his own fictional court case to create a new narrative: "A preparation derived from one page of Kafka passed through the student's brief and the original statement back and forth until a statement of biologic position emerges" (*Nova* 138). The resulting narrative reveals an underlying agenda in the defendant's (Life Form A's) original statement that justifies the act of parasiting Life Form B:

> Life Form A's room was on Ward Island—Crippled in such convenient Life Form B—Minraud an intricate door to cut off "oxygen" of life—Similar case operating through arrangements that could liquidate Life Form B by cutting off advocate from Minraud. (*Nova* 142)

Life Form A's original insistence on parasitism as "biologic need" is revealed to be an obfuscation of the underlying agenda to "liquidate Life Form B" (*Nova* 135). By disrupting the order and logic of a text, the fold-in exposes meanings buried within the structure of the language. Thus, the randomizing technique of the fold-in interrupts and reorders texts to create new and useful narratives and narrative forms.

Another cut-up section, "There's a Lot Ended," utilizes fragments presumably from newspaper stories to evoke many of the novel's themes. For example, the theme of resisting fixed identity is conveyed by the passage, "Definition of reasonable boy body between his denials—Identity popped in flash bulb breakfast" (*Nova* 168). Furthermore, the phrase "Both men had been neatly folded" (*Nova* 168) might suggest uniformity of identity, in the case of the men being individually folded into similar shapes; or conflation of identity, in the case that the two men are folded together into one. The form of the cut-up itself both raises and disrupts these themes, constantly restructuring the meaning(s) of the section. Through dynamic interaction with readers, such constantly evolving narratives are capable of triggering "the alteration of consciousness" (Doyle 240), and of "producing new kinds of subjectivities" (Hayles 217).

Both Burroughs and Serres recognize the parasite's productive as well as destructive potential. Serres advises that the parasite "exposes every system to ruin, it tends to exhaust reservoirs; it can kill everything it meets. But at the same time it multiplies the complexity which can be either suffocation or novelty; it excites production; it exalts and accelerates the exchanges of its hosts" (*Parasite* 187). And, as we have seen, the interplay between the destructive and productive functions of the parasite is essential to Burroughs's project of transformation and renewal through randomization. "Rupture is a necessary condition," as Murphy notes, "but by itself it is an insufficient condition for change" (172). The means for the system to reorder itself must also be present for change to occur. Burroughs's randomizing strategies provide both conditions: interrupting static repetition and creating opportunities for the autopoiesis of the narrative system. Indeed, for Burroughs the word parasite that can destroy the human host can also be used to "rewrite the message on 'the soft typewriter'" (*Ticket* 160). This final quotation from Serres could, in fact, serve as an epitaph for the body of Burroughs's experimental work: "It was only a noise, but it was also a message, a bit of information producing panic: an interruption, a corruption, a rupture of information. Was the noise really a message? Wasn't it, rather, static, a parasite? A parasite who has the last word, who produces disorder and who generates a different order" (*Parasite* 3).

Works Cited

Bales, Lawrence S. "Gregory Bateson, Cybernetics, and the Social/Behavioral Sciences." *Cybernetics & Human Knowing*, 3:1 (1995): 27-45. Print.

Bolton, Micheal Sean. "Digital Parasites: Reassessing Notions of Autonomy and Agency in Posthuman Subjectivity." *Theoria & Praxis: International Journal of Interdisciplinary Thought.* 1:2 (2013): 14-26. Print.

Brown, Steven D. and Paul Stenner. *Psychology Without Foundations: History, Philosophy and Psychosocial Theory*. Los Angeles: Sage, 2009. Print.

Burroughs, William S. *Cities of the Red Night.* New York: Henry Holt and Company, 1981. Print.

—. *Naked Lunch: The Restored Text*. New York: Grove P, 2001. Print.

—. *Nova Express*. New York: Grove P, 1964. Print.

—. *The Place of Dead Roads*. New York: Henry Holt and Company, 1983. Print.

—. *The Soft Machine*. New York: Grove P, 1966. Print.

—. *The Ticket That Exploded*. New York: Grove P, 1967. Print.

—. *The Western Lands*. New York: Viking, 1987. Print.

Doyle, Richard. "Naked Life: William S. Burroughs, Bioscientist." *Naked Lunch @ 50: Anniversary Essays*. Eds. Harris, Oliver and Ian MacFadyen. Carbondale: Southern Illinois UP, 2009. 238-49. Print.

Harris, Oliver. "Cutting Up Politics." *Retaking the Universe: William S. Burroughs in the Age of Globalization.* Eds. Davis Schneiderman and Philip Walsh. London: Pluto P, 2004. 175-200. Print.

Hayles, N. Katherine. *How We Became Posthuman: Virtual Bodies in Cybernetics, Literature, and Informatics*. Chicago: U of Chicago P, 1999. Print.

Hibbard, Allen ed. *Conversations with William S. Burroughs.* Jackson: UP of Mississippi, 1999. Print.

—. "Shift Coordinate Points: William S. Burroughs and Contemporary Theory." *Retaking the Universe: William S. Burroughs in the Age of Globalization.* Eds. Davis Schneiderman and Philip Walsh. London: Pluto P, 2004. 13- 28. Print.

Lydenberg, Robin. *Word Cultures: Radical Theory and Practice in William S. Burroughs' Fiction.* Urbana and Chicago: U of Illinois P, 1987. Print.

Murphy, Timothy S. *Wising Up the Marks: The Amodern William Burroughs.* Berkeley: U of California P, 1997. Print.

Nayar, Pramod K. *Posthumanism*. Cambridge: Polity P, 2014. Print.

Niebisch, Arndt. "Feedback: Media Parasites and the Circuits of Communication (Dada and Burroughs)." *Semiotic Review.* N.p. Issue 1 (April 2013): n. pag. Web. 19 May 2013.

Serres, Michel. *Genesis*. Trans. Geneviève James and James Nielson. Ann Arbor: U of Michigan P, 1995. (Trans. of Genèse. Paris: Grasset et Fasquelle, 1982). Print.

—. *The Parasite*. Trans. Lawrence R. Schehr. Minneapolis: U of Minnesota P, 2007. Print. (Trans. of Le Parasite. Paris: Grasset et Fasquelle, 1980). Print.

Shaviro, Steven. *Doom Patrols: A Theoretical Fiction about Postmodernism*. New York: Serpent's Tail, 1997. Print.

Skerl, Jennie. *William S. Burroughs*. Boston: Twayne P, 1985. Print.

Wolfe, Carey. "Bring the Noise: *The Parasite* and the Multiple Genealogies of Posthumanism." *The Parasite*. Minneapolis: U of Minnesota P, 2007. Print.

The Beats and Independent Film:
A Different Cast of Characters
Jane Falk

Soon after Allen Ginsberg returned to the United States in 1963, he wrote a piece for the *Times Literary Supplement* describing what was "happening now" in New York following his three-year absence: "Amazingly enough, MOVIES . . . I found on my return an excitement, a group, an art-gang, a society of friendly individuals who were running around the streets with home movie cameras taking each other's pictures just as—a decade ago—poets were running around . . . recording each other's vision in spontaneous language." He adds that "this is nothing like the commercial film of banks distributors money-stars etc. This is the film of cranks, eccentrics, sensitives, individuals one man one camera one movie . . . " (8). David James, in *Allegories of Cinema*, corroborates Ginsberg's impression: "Since the heyday of the beats, the baton of the preferred medium for subcultural mobilization has passed rapidly from writing to film and then to rock music" (348). James even categorizes some independent films of the 1960s as "Beat," with characteristics such as spontaneity, improvisation, sincerity, emphasis on the quotidian, and the inclusion of jazz and poetry. Such films also focused on countercultural types, such as Beat Generation characters whose transgressive behavior deviates from the norm.[1]

Just as Beat cultural values played a role in defining independent film production of the late 1950s and 1960s, so Beat writers themselves played a role in the filmmaking of this time period either as actors, writers, or producers of their own films. The first time the term "Beat" was applied to film may have been Parker Tyler's 1962 *Film Culture* review of the Robert Frank/Alfred Leslie film *Pull My Daisy,* with Jack Kerouac's film script and voice-over. Here Tyler describes "Beatism as a wee, wee cult," adding that it "is a collective form of authenticity" (109). The film, which won the second Independent Film Award of 1960, is a day in the life of a group of bohemians played by real life Beat writers Allen Ginsberg and Gregory Corso, along with Peter Orlovsky, who hang out at the pad of a railway man, Milo, with his wife and child.[2] At the film and day's end, Milo's pals leave, taking Milo with them, his wife in tears. The Beat types offer a contrast with the more middle class values of Milo's wife and that day's guests: a bishop, his mother, and sister. This, however, was only one of a number of such collaborations, which exhibited certain characteristics in common. Beat poets and independent filmmakers shared the same social and artistic scene (Stan Brakhage met Michael McClure through Robert Duncan); published in each other's magazines (McClure and ruth weiss in *Film Culture*); and experienced almost constant censorship during this time (for example, McClure and Lenore Kandel for their writing).

A number of critical studies have appeared on the subject of Beat writers and independent film. Among the most well-known are David Sterritt's books, *Mad to be Saved* and *Screening the Beats*, along with Daniel Kane's *We Saw the Light* and Jack Sargeant's *Naked Lens*. In looking at such texts, one might say that independent film has been dominated by the masculine, an emphasis that has not changed much over the years. In his 1967 study, *An Introduction to the American Underground Film*, Sheldon Renan claims that the mid-century underground film "issued from a volatile environment . . . the climate of the new man." He goes on to explain this phenomenon of the "fifties" as a "willful withdrawal from cooperation with contemporary goals and modes of living. One example of this was the passive nonconformity of the Beats . . ." (42). Ironically, however, a number of Beat participants in the underground film culture of the time were women. In this regard, this essay presents both an expanded yet more focused view of independent film with a slightly different cast of characters, specifically women. As actors, women were given somewhat objectified roles, while as filmmakers themselves they provided roles in which women were empowered and at times dominant.

One aspect of this argument is the way male and female actors are treated differently by independent filmmakers. While male Beat writers were often presented as themselves, at times in the act of reading their poetry, their female counterparts usually appear in underground narratives where they are sexualized or take part in somewhat transgressive behaviors.[3] For example, Stan Brakhage creates film portraits of his poet friends Robert Creeley and Michael McClure in *Two: Creeley/McClure,* part of *15 Song Traits* (1965), a series that also included the Zukofsky and Dorn families. The visual effects of these short home movies are experimental, with ghostly superimpositions and jagged and dynamic camera movement. These act as devices of rhyme and rhythm with recurrent motifs such as a focus on the poets's hands as symbolic gestures. The aim, according to Brakhage, was to demonstrate the personalities and work of the subjects through film, even though the films are silent.[4] In both cases, Creeley and McClure are the centerpieces and the center of attention of the camera eye.[5]

In contrast, women poets are presented in more shocking and transgressive roles. For example, Diane di Prima plays the role of scantily clad Pregnant Cutie in Jack Smith's *Normal Love* (1963). Di Prima grew up in Brooklyn and associated both with the Beat Generation and the Lower East Side avant-garde of the 1950s and 1960s. Smith and di Prima shared the same cultural milieu. Smith had published a prose poem, "Normal Love," in di Prima and LeRoi Jones's *The Floating Bear* and had shown his films at di Prima's Poets Theatre. In addition, they both had been censored for their work: di Prima for her editing of *The Floating Bear* and Smith for his films. According to di Prima, the Poets Theatre "turned the week nights over to various other programs," among which was Jonas Mekas's Cinematheque (377). It was in February and March 1964, according to J. Hoberman's account, that Smith's production slides of *Normal Love* and Smith's film *Flaming Creatures* were the targets of police raids at the Poets Theatre's New Bowery Theater location (42).

Normal Love was ostensibly about monsters from horror films in a phantasmagoric natural setting, with one long section featuring a beautiful woman handling a python. The film presents a languorous, sensual, and perverse world replete with camp monsters, transvestites, and the semi-nude. Smith asked di Prima to take part in the film, and she appears in the finale, which features a gigantic cake upon which a tableau of scantily clad dancing girls protect one of the main characters, Pink Fairy. There are numerous close-ups of di Prima's pregnant belly. In her memoirs of these years, *Recollections of My Life as a Woman*, di Prima describes her part as to "dance vigorously on the lowest tier of said cake, a print skirt tied under my huge belly . . . and tiny pasties on my nipples" (359). She adds that at the sight of the Green Mummy, "We screamed and fainted or did something of the sort. We all fell off the cake in any case, feigning various campy approximations of terror" (360). Unfortunately, the film was never completed and had primarily private screenings as rushes and rough cuts through 1965, according to Hoberman (96). Hence, it did not have the same opportunity to be banned as Smith's infamous *Flaming Creatures*.

Interestingly, di Prima also appeared with her then-husband Alan Marlowe in one of Andy Warhol's short portrait films of 1964, *Alan Marlowe/Diane di Prima*, discussed by Reva Wolf in her study of Warhol.[6] Wolf quotes di Prima, who had contacted Warhol suggesting that he "come see us & shoot a Day in Our House like you said & show Alan & me pornography." The action takes place in the couple's bedroom, as di Prima recalls: "Alan is in bed, and he's covered by a tiger skin, which he's stroking the tail of in a very obviously suggestive manner. I get on the bed in a black leotard and tights and kind of trample him. It was a tiny room" (qtd. in Wolf 44). This film's sexual overtone upends traditional roles with Marlowe as the seemingly passive, semi-nude figure and di Prima as the more active, clothed partner. Going against sexual mores of the time and creating "pornography" appears to be as much a part of di Prima's avant-garde anti-bourgeois shock tactics as those of Warhol.[7]

Lenore Kandel, associated with the Bay Area poetry scene, the hippie movement in San Francisco's Haight Ashbury, and the Beat movement, also appeared in independent film.[8] She plays the Deaconess, a mystic visionary associated with a Satanic cult, in Kenneth Anger's *Invocation of My Demon Brother* (1969). Her role, in comparison to di Prima's, is not so much sexually shocking as it is shocking to Christian sensibility. This short, eleven-minute film, cuts between footage from a Satanic Ritual of the Equinox presided over by Kenneth Anger as Magus in 1967

San Francisco Haight Ashbury combined with images of nude men, an albino, Anger's tattoos, Deacon, Deaconess, a burning cat, drugs, the Devil, and Marines landing in helicopters. Footage of the Rolling Stones in concert shot in London a year later was subsequently added, and the film was completed in 1969. Toward the beginning of the film, Kandel appears as Deaconess, with others smoking marijuana through a skull pipe; later bearing a goldfish bowl, she processes with the same group down a stairway.[9] Anger claims the film was his reaction to the war in Vietnam; in addition the superimposed and multiple camera images seem intended to invoke the mood of the drug experience of LSD or magic mushrooms.[10] The ritual itself recalls that of mystic and Satanist Aleister Crowley, who Anger admired. In an interview with Scott MacDonald, Anger describes the ceremony: "For *Invocation* I performed a Crowley ceremony,'The Equinox of the Gods,' to commemorate the autumn equinox, at the Straight Theater in the Haight-Ashbury, in 1967. I had someone [Ben Van Meter] film it for me, since I was involved in the ritual" (45).

There is no record of when Anger asked Kandel to be part of the film, but their paths had crossed at various alternative events in San Francisco, including the January 1967 "Human Be-In" and the February 1967 Glide Memorial Church "Invisible Circus." In the same MacDonald interview, Anger notes that he "met several of the characters…in the Haight-Ashbury" (45). While the Deaconess is not usually a role associated with this ritual, Anger may have added it to include Kandel because with her *Love Book* (published 1966, banned 1967), she had achieved some notoriety for explicit language and subject matter. Its cover shows a couple in tantric embrace, alluding to the kind of sexual magic Anger strove to invoke with his films. *Invocation of My Demon Brother* actually includes images of superimposed nude lovers, with the superimposition making the imagery less obvious to most viewers. Thus, her appearance could be considered part of the magical law of correspondences.[11] In addition, Kandel's then-boyfriend, a Hell's Angel named Sweet William, played the role of the Deacon, so Anger may have felt it appropriate to include her. After completion, the film was widely shown. As Bill Landis notes in his 1969 biography of Anger, it was "enthusiastically received on the underground film circuit in the United States." He adds that this film and others would "jump-start the phenomenon of cult movies" (175).

A more significant aspect of female participation in independent films is that of women as filmmakers, writing and directing their films themselves. The earliest of these was ruth weiss's *The Brink* (1961). A German émigré, weiss was a poet on the North Beach scene, intersecting with Beat writers such as Jack Kerouac. She was also an early proponent of reading poetry to jazz. *The Brink* was shot in and around San Francisco by painter Paul Beattie, who had asked weiss to write a script for a film, for which she used her poem, "The Brink" (1960).[12] She also chose locations for the film, edited it, and added a jazz sound score and voice-over of her poems.

The Brink is the story of two main characters, young lovers referred to as *he* and *she*, their relationship presented over several days and in various locations. The film credits show a caterpillar inching its way over a white surface, then action moves to Bay Area locations such as a city café, the beach, a cottage, Chinatown, a park with satyr statue, a forest, Playland at the Beach amusement park, and a housing development under construction. Toward the end of the film, the lovers are in a vacant lot where *he* puts a bracelet made of a dried snake skin on *she*. The couple then moves to a mailbox where they find a collage with a caterpillar crawling on it, a return to the film's beginning and the suggestion that the caterpillar may soon transform into a butterfly. Perhaps finding the collage indicates the part that art has to play in balancing opposing forces of male and female. The caterpillar is symbolic, as a poem of weiss's featured on the VHS/DVD cover makes clear: "it can crawl to the brink / but it cannot yet fly" (3-4). The poem ends with the concept of transformation:

>   And the he and she fearing love as completion
>   Call forth all interference
>   This until the simple point of contact
>   Where the butterfly is possible. (10-13)

Film Still from *The Brink*; Courtesy of the artist

This film might be considered an example of what P. Adams Sitney characterizes as mythopoeic film in his study *Visionary Cinema*, with images which "are not so much symbolic as archetypal, drawn primarily from the visual vocabulary of ancient mythology" (30).[13] Mythopoeia seems to relate to the "preoccupations" of Jung rather than to those of Freud (31). In an earlier essay published in *Film Culture*, "Imagism in Four Avant-Garde Films," Sitney considers that "mythopoeia is the often attempted and seldom achieved result of making a myth new or making a new myth" (199). In weiss's film, *he* and *she* appear as archetypal figures of lovers, a modern version of Adam and Eve in the Garden of Eden, although weiss's lovers appear as equals rather than as the female being subordinate to the male. *She* leads him as often as *he* leads her. *She* appears dominant in a scene at the Bay's edge where *she* splashes him and then drags him into the water. The equality of the sexes is an important aspect of *The Brink,* as pointed out by Nancy M. Grace in *Breaking the Rule of Cool: Interviewing and Reading Women Beat Writers*: "[T]he film augments the vision of Beat culture, representing a heterogenous egalitarianism that counters the misogyny of the 1959 Robert Frank/Alfred Leslie film *Pull My Daisy*" (58).[14]

Elements of the surreal are another aspect of this film, specifically in the eccentric and sometimes illogical juxtapositions of the action, including scenes with dreamlike qualities hinting at the subconscious mind of the characters.[15] The film's editing at times presents viewers with abrupt and seemingly irrational scene changes. For example, action shifts from the lovers and a group of friends eating a meal at the beach house to a scene where *she* walks the streets of Chinatown described by the voice over as a "won ton woman, wanton woman." In another sequence, *he* is suddenly alone in his flat and lies down to sleep. The scene shifts to daytime with the lovers in a park where they encounter a headless satyr statue, after which they are shown lying in the grass appearing to wake up. What has been dreamt? Who has been dreaming?

Another aspect of the film that seems important to weiss is the emphasis on the natural world, which a refrain from "The Brink" reinforces:

> to clean water use earth
> to clean earth use fire
> to clean fire use air
> to clean air
> enter.[16] (245-249)

These lines are voiced over scenes of water, sky, and bird life. The natural world also recalls haiku poetry, a genre important to weiss.[17] Stan Brakhage made note of the film's affinity with haiku in letters from California published in *Film Culture,* Summer 1963, stating that the film attempts "to pitch the actors into situations preordained by ruth weiss's poetry yet leave them free of the context unaware of the poetic narrative intended, to develop synthesis of poetry and image highly structured but containing a residue of very real immediate, almost haiku feeling" (80). Shortly after its completion, weiss showed her film to Brakhage at his home, and it was subsequently screened at Canyon Cinema and the 1961 San Francisco International Film Festival.[18]

In contrast, Helen Adam's *Daydream of Darkness* (1963) is less a "mainstream" version of an independent film (if such is not an oxymoronic term) than her own idiosyncratic vision and embodiment of her poems, "Anaid Si Taerg (Great is Diana)" and "Daydream of Darkness." In both poems, the moon plays a starring role. A Scots émigré, Adam was a balladeer and performance poet who was part of the San Francisco Renaissance in the 1950s and 1960s, closely connected with Robert Duncan's circle. Adam asked painter Bill McNeill to collaborate on this film with her. According to Lewis Ellingham and Kevin Killian in their study of Jack Spicer, Adam wrote the script and chose the images while McNeill produced and directed, and both worked on the editing of the film. *Daydream of Darkness* was originally presented as silent with Adam performing the voice-over to musical accompaniment.

Film Still from *Daydream of Darkness,* copyright the Poetry Collection of the University Libraries, University at Buffalo, The State University of New York and used with permission

The heroine of the film is the Moon Goddess, Diana, present as a metal relief sculpture: a large round disk with a woman's head framed by a crescent moon. It is placed in various natural settings, most often at the beach.[19] Women are also privy to the "world's mysteries," as the voice-over contends. Other male and female god and goddess figures appear as art nouveau statues brandished almost as if they were hand puppets, but only rarely are the hands of the "puppeteers" visible. The statues along with images of Adam's collages alternate with more dynamic scenes of two couples, one bearing candles in a domestic setting, the other emerging from and merging with the ocean. Adam appears as a seer holding up tarot cards of Lovers, the Devil, and the Moon. The high point emotionally may be the lovers kissing in a salt marsh. The film's final image is of a stone face falling off of a book on Voodoo, preceded by the lovers walking in the sea swept apart by waves. The juxtaposition of the lovers with the Voodoo head presents an inexplicable and surreal ending reinforced by the lyric script with the following lines accompanying these actions: "LOVE AND LONELINESS NEVER EXISTED NO! NO! LET ME CLING TO A TEAR OR A RAIN DROP TERRIBLE ARE THE TRUTHS OF ZEN" (264).[20] The juxtaposition of moon worship, Voodoo, and Zen is an additional surreal touch.[21]

This film is another example of the mythopoeic with emphasis on the mythic and archetypal. The words of the songs, poems, and script invoke Diana, Huntress and Goddess of the Moon, while presenting love between men and women as often doomed, a fate exemplified in these lines: "BUT SHE COULDNA HA' BECKONED MY LOVE TAE THE FIRE…HAD HE NEVER BEEN FALSE TAE ME" (262). The last sections of the script make allusions to Buddhist concepts of the Void and emptiness: "THE VOID ALONE IS REAL…EVERYTHING IS NOTHING… LOVE…AND LONELINESS…NEVER EXISTED" (263-64).[22] Perhaps Adam is suggesting that the futility of love and desire represented in the ballad tradition is similar to the Buddhist concepts of the Four Noble Truths, the second of which is that desire is the cause of suffering.[23] In a technological age when men are preparing to land on the moon, the moon herself seems doomed. The following lines of the film script, however, suggest that the Moon remains powerful and can overcome opposites: "AND THERE SHALL BE NO MORE MOONLIGHT. AND THERE SHALL BE NO MORE MOONLIGHT…AND THERE SHALL BE NO MORE OPPOSITES OVER ALL THE EARTH" (260). Despite this somewhat negative ending, the film's lasting impression is one of female dominance and identification with the natural world.[24] It is unclear how often the film was shown after its premiere in 1963 at The Peacock Gallery, San Francisco. Adam did not make another film, but concentrated on reprising her musical, *San Francisco's Burning*, after leaving San Francisco and moving to New York.

A third female independent filmmaker is Joanne Kyger. Moving to North Beach in the 1950s from Santa Barbara, she became associated with both the San

Francisco Renaissance and the Beat Generation. An experimental video, not a film, Kyger's *Descartes* (1967), was made in conjunction with the National Center for Experiments in Television (NCET), San Francisco.[25] Kyger wrote her poem, "Descartes and the Splendor Of," as a "screenplay" for the video. She was asked to participate in this project on her return to the Bay Area from a stay in New York from 1966-67, and considers *Descartes* her most successful and finished work for the project. Interestingly, she had been a stand-in for a Jack Smith film, *Mr. President,* and had met Andy Warhol and seen his film *Chelsea Girls,* so experimental film was part of her background at this time. A seeming parody or deconstruction of Enlightenment philosopher René Descartes's *Discourse on Method,* the video is for Kyger an "adaptation."[26]

Kyger's poem and video rewrite and revise Descartes's *Discourse* from a female point of view; in the process He becomes She, and God becomes Mother God. It is a poem and film in six parts, the first of which shows Kyger beginning a journey with a close-up of her face and a newsreel-like review of contemporary life. The second and third parts present the narrator/Descartes in a domestic setting sweeping and mending, as she literalizes his admonition to sweep out old ideas from the mind. In the fourth part, her head takes up the full screen again as she intones Descartes's famous words: "I THINK hence I AM. OR I doubt hence I Am; or I reject hence I am. You get the picture." The fifth part presents Mother God as a hieratic goddess figure distorted by camera effects of multiple image and superimposition. A fanfare sounds. The last part returns to a contemporary scene in the TV studio, the camera focused in on the narrator/Descartes and her final revelations. The video ends with the narrator's curtsey to Mother God, as she speaks the poem's last line: "ONE CANNOT SO WELL LEARN A THING WHEN IT HAS BEEN LEARNED FROM ANOTHER, AS WHEN ONE HAS DISCOVERED IT HIMSELF."[27] However, the video's final move is the narrator's correction of that last line; she follows the poem's (and Descartes's) word, *himself,* with the added word, *herself.*

For Kyger, video seemed an apt medium with which to deconstruct Descartes's ideas about mind/body duality. As she put it, Descartes's "body mind problem could be resolved in videospace."[28] Video was an open field in which the aural and the visual could meet and merge; experimenting in another medium other than language could express the idea of ridding oneself of mind/body duality. The video also positions Kyger in the mythopoeic tradition. Descartes's God is replaced by a vision of Mother God as goddess figure, enhanced by visual and aural feedback. Kyger moves her arms up and down, her appearance similar to that of Diana the Many-Breasted, as her voice echoes and reverberates.[29] Enhanced by electronic distortion and feedback, these vocal and tonal shifts are among the most remarkable of the video's aspects. Her voice ranges from that of a humorous cartoon character to an authoritarian, professorial mode, and then to the other-worldly voice of Mother God, ending with what might be Kyger's own voice. She notes that the sound track and voice changes were created collaboratively with composer Richard Felciano: "Each of the six parts of *Descartes* had a different video set and a different sound and vocal approach."[30] The completed video was subsequently shown on San Francisco broadcast television in November 1968.[31]

Film Still from *Descartes*; Courtesy of the artist

In making these films and videos, women poets created not just lyrical film poems or a type of experimental film, but films which enhance their poetry. Film provides what Kyger considers an expanded field in which to work. The imagery of the films augments that of the poems and was a way for these filmmakers to represent Pound's early twentieth-century imagism. For example, images of the goddess in various configurations and in various physical spaces in Adam's *Daydream of Darkness* provide various ideas of what the goddess means to men and women. Imagism in the context of film is a term used by Sitney in his essay, "Imagism in Four Avant-Garde Films." His influence in using this term was Ezra Pound's imagist manifesto, and Sitney cites a passage from this text as the epigraph to his essay: "The image is not an idea. It is a radiant node or cluster" (187).[32] In "A Few Don'ts," the text in which Pound originally presented the term, he explains, "An 'Image' is that which presents an intellectual and emotional complex in an instant of time" (4).[33] By imagism, Sitney means that the camera concentrates "on a single human and one significant action" (190). Imagism can also include themes related to that image, especially when the image bears mythopoeic overtones. One central image can motivate an entire film, as demonstrated by Adam's moon goddess in *Daydream of Darkness* or weiss's lovers who wander through various scenes in *The Brink*. As the action proceeds, more of the complex relationship of the lovers is revealed. Even though none of these examples corresponds to a single human's one significant action, a connection to Sitney's theories is evident, especially considering his comment in *Visionary Cinema* that "lateral or foreign material is introduced around the essential action without completely disrupting its unity or continuity" (26).

Another way film work expanded these poets' existing interests was by reinforcing the oral and performative aspects of their work: weiss as jazz poet and Adam as balladeer. Kyger would be further influenced by her video to emphasize tone of voice in poetry as she notes in a 1977 interview.[34] In regard to improvisation, another aspect of the performative, of the three poem scripts, weiss's treatment is the most improvisatory and least like a straightforward reading, as she breaks up "The Brink" to fit the action of the film. Kyger's vocal distortions impart an improvisatory quality to the reading of her poem. In comparison, it is unclear how Adam's voice-over changed or whether she improvised. She may have sung her lines, but there is no recording of her performance. Note that di Prima and Kandel do not speak in their films, and, in fact, independent films of the time were often silent with musical accompaniment. Perhaps the poets' voice-overs were an unconscious response to the silent voices of other experimental filmmakers and to women in experimental film in general.

The women involved in these projects worked primarily before the feminist wave of the 1970s when problems of women's stereotypes were being actively addressed. As actors in films by men, they chose to be associated with transgressive and non-conformist film statements, which were not necessarily feminist but at least demonstrated that women were able to choose such roles. Di Prima shows her pregnant belly without shame, a statement of fecund sexuality. In *Alan Marlowe/ Diane di Prima*, she is the active sexual partner. As filmmakers, women dominate the action and all women act in their films, as well as perform voice-overs, from weiss's bit part to Kyger's starring role.[35] Instead of appropriated female bodies, they present archetypal images that are more often dominant over the male (Kyger's Mother God) or at least equal (weiss's *he* and *she*), with emphasis on the close connection between the female and forces of nature (Adam's Moon Goddess, Diana). The interest in the mythic often features feminist symbols or female goddesses, as when God is replaced by Mother God in *Descartes*.

Emphasis on the feminine aspects of the mythopoeic suggests that these films were feminist statements before their time. However, problems with the stereotyping of women are evident in the use of the mythopoeic, as noted by Dianne Sadoff in her essay "Mythopoeia, The Moon, and Contemporary Women's Poetry": "The landscape of our mythology reflects masculine activity and female passivity …Woman becomes passive nature, man its active and heroic inhabitant" (96). Focusing on moon mythology, she writes, "Whether wife, Great Mother, sacred prostitute, or virgin, then, sexuality is central to the moon goddess's identity and to worship of her" (97). For Sadoff, the feminist solution to stereotyping is transformation: "When a woman writer encounters these mythologies, she must reinvent, revise, and transform them to fit…her unique female experience. Contemporary women poets correct dualistic moon myths by reexamining both aspects of the moon goddess, the virgin and the prostitute" (98).

Whether weiss, Adam, or Kyger achieved this transformation remains to be decided by twenty-first-century viewers. Adam, for example, could have played into lunar stereotypes as much as she transformed them. The moon is the female and the sun is the male in these lines from the lyric script of *Daydream of Darkness*: "THE LORDLY SUN IN THE HEAVENS MOVE" (259). In her poem "Anaid si taerg (Great is Diana)," which serves as partial basis for the film, the male is active—"Man's alive, he's got what it takes" (24)—while the moon seems doomed: "Horns, horns, blow for the moon's mort" (34).

Of all the films discussed, *Descartes* can be considered the closest to a feminist film statement, as David James's reference to Julia Lesage's discussion of feminist consciousness-raising film projects suggests: "Within such a narrative structure, either a single woman tells her story…or a group of women are filmed sharing experiences in a politicized way. They are filmed in domestic space in a 'new woman-identified way'" (323). Although Kyger does not claim objectivity in her "adaptation" of Descartes and does not use a documentary structure; her film presents a domestic space in a "new woman-identified way." As well, the film presents Mother God, a powerful, feminist figure. At the very least, a discussion of these films reminds us that though under-represented in critical discussion of independent Beat films of the mid-twentieth century, women were active participants in the scene. They used their own voices and their own film scripts, or rewrote male-authored texts.

We now conclude with a consideration of the liberatory possibilities of independent film itself. For Walter Benjamin, in "The Work of Art in the Age of Mechanical Reproduction," film has power to direct attention to details of daily life sometimes missed or overlooked: "By close-ups of the things around us, by focusing on hidden details of familiar objects, by exploring common place milieus under the ingenious guidance of the camera, the film, on the one hand, extends our comprehension of the necessities which rule our lives; on the other hand, it manages to assure us of an immense and unexpected field of action" (236). In the space between the words and images in these women-authored films and in their focus on relationships, can what Judith Butler calls the destabilizing of "naturalized categories of identity" (139) occur? Can female stereotypes be transformed? Writing as a contemporary of these filmmakers, Herbert Marcuse in his 1964 study *One-Dimensional Man: Studies in the Ideology of Advanced Industrial Society* suggests they can: "The aesthetic dimension still retains a freedom of expression which enables the writer and artist to call men and things by their name—to name the otherwise unnameable" (247). As actors or filmmakers, women are no longer only passive recipients of the male gaze, but active participants in the making of their own films, presenting relationships between the sexes from a woman's point of view.

Notes

[1] See James Chapter 4, first section, "Film and the Beat Generation." Note that in this essay, I use the term "independent film" for this phenomenon, although other terms such as *New American Cinema* (recalling New American Poetry), visionary film, underground film, experimental film, avant-garde film, or alternative film are also in circulation. See James and Sheldon Renan for more on these terms.

[2] This award was established by Jonas Mekas in his magazine *Film Culture*, the most significant publication of the independent film scene at the time.

[3] Some exceptions are narratives in which male Beats appear, such as Lew Welch in *The Great Blondino*, Michael McClure in *Beyond the Law*, or Allen Ginsberg in *Me and My Brother*. The actors are not sexualized, although Ginsberg and his lover, Peter Orlovsky, appear in *Me and My Brother*, as well as in Gregory Markopoulos's film, *Galaxie*. McClure's character's sexuality is emphasized at times.

[4] Guy Davenport describes the McClure film as "a raging flash of faces, some of which are the lion's face McClure assumes for the readings; Robert Creeley, also in black and white, and frequently in negative, an evocation of the poet's tense sincerity" (11).

[5] Another film portrait of a poet is *Liberty Crown*, Bruce Connor's video of McClure reading his poetry, which is apparently now lost. Even in Frank's film *Me and My Brother*, Ginsberg reads his poetry.

[6] Although *Marlow/Diane di Prima* was listed as a screen test in Warhol's film catalogue, Warhol Museum curator Greg Pierce considers that short portrait film best describes this work.

[7] For example, Warhol's 1964 film, *Couch*, includes sex acts as well as nudity; interestingly, one of its vignettes features Beat writers Kerouac, Ginsberg, and Orlovsky cavorting but clothed on said Factory couch, a possible allusion to *Pull My Daisy*.

[8] Kandel also had a relationship with poet Lew Welch and appears as Ramona Schwartz in Kerouac's novel *Big Sur*.

[9] William Wees in *Light Moving in Time* suggests that she may be patterned after Crowley's *Scarlet Woman,* a priestess with sexual associations (120).

[10] This commentary can be found on the DVD version of Anger's *The Complete Magick Lantern Cycle*.

[11] *A Dictionary of Symbols* describes this law as "founded upon the assumption that all cosmic phenomena are limited and serial and that they appear as scales or series on separate planes . . . the components of one series are linked with those of another in their essence and in their ultimate significance" (60).

[12] According to a telephone interview with weiss, this poem was used along with lines from other poems, including "Chop Sticks" and those in *Blue in Green*.

[13] Ray Carney, in his essay "Escape Velocity: Notes on Beat Film," also characterizes weiss as an "allegorical or symbolic" artist (207).

[14] According to weiss, she was unfamiliar with this film at the time she made *The Brink*.

[15] Note Grace's discussion of surrealism in conjunction with weiss in "ruth weiss's DESERT JOURNAL: a Modern-Beat-Pomo Performance" in *Reconstructing the Beats*. Ed. Jennie Skerl. New York, NY: Palgrave-Macmillan, 2004.

[16] Quotations from "The Brink" are taken from weiss's *Single Out*.

[17] weiss notes in an interview in *Breaking the Rule of Cool* that she wrote haiku in North Beach with Jack Kerouac in the 1950s (64).

[18] In *The Brink*, weiss makes a cameo appearance as a fellow transit passenger on the bus with the couple.

[19] According to M. Esther Harding in *Woman's Mysteries,* "Diana, the Huntress, was none other than the Moon Goddess, Mother of all animals. She is shown in her statues crowed with the crescent . . ." (130). A Roman goddess, she is identified with the Greek Artemis. ruth weiss has a poem to Diana and her temple in her first collection, *Blue in Green.*

[20] Page numbers refer to the published lyric script in *A Helen Adam Reader*.

[21] Adam probably ended the film with these lines. In reproducing the film for the DVD of the *Helen Adam Reader*, Kristin Prevallet added a voice-over of Adam's original script and music to the originally silent film. However, not all the script as it appears in the *Reader* has been included in the DVD version; these last lines are among those left out.

[22] Note that Prevallet has left these lines out of the new version of the film, as well as lines mentioning Zen.

[23] The Four Noble Truths include the truth of suffering; the cause of that suffering in desire; there is a way to deal with that cause; and the truth of the cessation of suffering is the Eightfold Path. According to Prevallet in an email dated January 31, 2015, to the author of this essay, there is no explicit connection between Adam and Buddhism, except that it was part of the cultural conversation of the time.

[24] Prevallet in her essay "The Worm Queen Emerges" claims that ballads are liberatory for women (29).

[25] Gene Youngblood, in his study *Expanded Cinema*, considers experimental video to be an outgrowth of experimental film, and James likens non-commercial video to an "aesthetic project parallel to that of structural film" (350).

[26] This quote and the one above indicate Kyger's characterization of her work, according to her email of May 21, 2015.

[27] This is the line as published in *Places To Go*, the basis for the video, which Kyger added during filming. Capitalized words in the poem indicate quotes or close quotes from Descartes. The passage from Descartes reads in part in the original as follows: "that there may not be in the world many minds incomparably superior to my own, but because no one can so well understand a thing and make it his own when learnt from another as when it is discovered for himself" (124).

[28] This quote is from an email to the author of January 20, 2006.

[29] For an image of this goddess, see Harding's *Woman's Mysteries* (108).

[30] Quote from an email from Kyger dated May 26, 2015. Note that Felciano was composer for the NCET video project.

[31] Kyger's video was also featured in UC Berkeley's *Videospace* exhibition of 2001 and included in the Getty Museum *California Video* exhibition of 2008.

[32] Sitney credits Stan Brakhage's interest in Pound's imagism as his influence in developing this idea.

[33] "A Few Don'ts" was originally published in *Poetry* in 1913.

[34] See Kyger's interview for *Credences* in which she considers the poem as a "score for the voice" (64).

[35] Their acting and voice-overs are similar to those of William S. Burroughs in his films, especially *Towers Open Fire*.

Works Cited

Adam, Helen. *A Helen Adam Reader*. Ed. Kristin Prevallet. Orono, Maine: The National Poetry Foundation, 2007. Print.

Alan Marlowe/Diane di Prima. Dir. Andy Warhol. 1964. Orig. 16 mm. DVD.

Anger, Kenneth. "Kenneth Anger." Interview by Scott MacDonald. *A Critical Cinema 5*. Ed. Scott MacDonald. Berkeley: U of California P, 2006. 16-54. Print.
Benjamin, Walter. "The Work of Art in the Age of Mechanical Reproduction." *Illuminations*. Ed. Hannah Arendt. Trans. Harry Zohn. New York: Schocken Books, 1968. 217-51. Print.
Brakhage, Stan. "Letters: San Francisco Film Scene." *Film Culture*. 29 (Summer 1963): 76-102. Print.
The Brink. Dir. ruth weiss. Camera: Paul Beattie. 1961. Orig. 16 mm. DVD.
Butler, Judith. *Gender Trouble*. New York: Routledge, 1990. Print.
Carney, Ray. "Escape Velocity: Notes on Beat Film." *Beat Culture and the New America*: 1950-1965. Ed. Lisa Phillips. New York: Whitney Museum of American Art, 1995. 190-209. Print.
Cirlot, J. E. "Correspondences." *A Dictionary of Symbols*. Trans. Jack Sage. New York: Philosophical Library, 1962. Print.
Creeley/McClure: Two Songs. Dir.: Stan Brakhage. 1965. Orig. 16 mm. DVD.
Davenport, Guy. "Two Essays on Brakhage and His Songs: Guy Davenport." *Film Culture*. 40 (Spring 1966): 9-12. Print.
Daydream of Darkness. Dir.: Helen Adam. Camera: William McNeill. 1963. Orig. 16mm. DVD.
Descartes. Dir.: Joanne Kyger. Camera: Loren Sears. Videotape. 1968.
Descartes, René. *The Philosophical Works of Descartes*. Trans. Elizabeth Haldane and G.R.T. Ross. Vol. I. New York: Dover Publications, 1955. Print.
Di Prima, Diane. *Recollections of My Life as a Woman*. New York: Viking, 2001. Print.
Ellingham, Lewis, and Kevin Killian. *Poet Be Like God: Jack Spicer and the San Francisco Renaissance*. Hanover and London: Wesleyan UP, 1998. Print.
Ginsberg, Allen. "Back to the Wall." *Deliberate Prose: Selected Essays 1952-1995*. Ed. Bill Morgan. New York: HarperCollins, 2001. 6-9. Print.
Harding, M. Esther. *Woman's Mysteries*. New York: Pantheon Books, 1955. Print.
Hill, Jerome, and Guy Davenport. "Two Essays on Brakhage and His Songs." *Film Culture*. 40 (Summer 1966): 8-12. Print.
Hoberman, J. *On Jack Smith's* Flaming Creatures *and Other Secret-Flix of Cinemaroc*. New York: Hips Road, 2001. Print.
Invocation of My Demon Brother. Dir. Kenneth Anger. 1969. Orig. 16mm. DVD.
James, David. *Allegories of Cinema*. New York: E. P. Dutton, 1970. Print.
Kyger, Joanne. Email to author. 15 January 2015.
—. Email to author. 22 May 2015.
—. Email to author. 26 May 2015.
—. *Places To Go*. Los Angeles: Black Sparrow, 1970. Print.

—. "Three Versions of the Poetic Line." *Credences*. 2.1 (March 1977): 55-66. Print.
Landis, Bill. *Anger: The Unauthorized Biography of Kenneth Anger*. New York: HarperCollins, 1995. Print.
Marcuse, Herbert. *One-Dimensional Man: Studies in the Ideology of Advanced Industrial Society*. Boston: Beacon, 1964. Print.
Normal Love. Dir.: Jack Smith. 1963-64. 16 mm.
Pierce, Greg. Telephone interview with the author. 20 December 2015.
Pound, Ezra. *Literary Essays of Ezra Pound*. Ed. T.S. Eliot. New York: New Directions, 1968. 3-14. Print.
Prevallet, Kristin. Email to author. 31 January 2015.
—. "The Worm Queen Emerges." *Girls Who Wore Black*. Ed. Ronna C. Johnson and Nancy M. Grace. New Brunswick, NJ: Rutgers U P, 2002. 25-44. Print.
Renan, Sheldon. *An Introduction to the American Underground Film*. New York: E.P. Dutton, 1967. Print.
Sadoff, Dianne. "Mythopoeia, The Moon, and Contemporary Women's Poetry." *The Massachusetts Review*. XIX.1 (1978): 93-110. Print.
Sitney, P. Adams. "Imagism in Four Avant-Garde Films." *Film Culture Reader*. Ed. P. Adams Sitney. New York: Praeger, 1970. 187-200. Print.
—. *Visionary Cinema*. New York: Oxford UP, 1974. Print.
Tyler, Parker. "For *Shadows*, Against *Pull My Daisy*." *Film Culture Reader*. Ed. P. Adams Sitney. New York: Praeger, 1970. 108-117. Print.
Wees, William C. *Light Moving in Time*. Berkeley: U of California P, 1992. Print.
weiss, ruth. *Blue in Green*. San Francisco: Adler Press, 1960. Print.
—. *Single Out*. Mill Valley, CA: D'Aurora, 1978. Print.
—. "Single Out." Interview by Nancy M. Grace. *Breaking the Rule of Cool*. Ed. Nancy M. Grace and Ronna C. Johnson. Jackson: UP of Mississippi, 2004. 55-80. Print.
—. Telephone interview with the author. 13 February 2015.
—. Telephone interview with the author. 11 May 2015.
Wolf, Reva. *Andy Warhol: Poetry, and Gossip in the 1960s*. Chicago: U of Chicago P, 1997. Print.
Youngblood, Gene. *Expanded Cinema*. New York: E. P. Dutton, 1970. Print.

Allen Ginsberg's Ambivalent Whitman
Anne Lovering Rounds

> *Where are we going, Walt Whitman?*
> —Allen Ginsberg, "A Supermarket in California"

Where *is* Allen Ginsberg going with Walt Whitman? The question at the start of the final stanza of "A Supermarket in California" is deceptively simple, suggesting the poem's premise of exchange or experience in a common location—a supermarket, a street, a city, state, or country—as the basis for the two poets' relationship. But as it unfolds, the last stanza reveals a more difficult line of inquiry: not where but in what way Ginsberg shares in Whitman's expansive, celebratory worldview and in the seminal features of poems that express such a perspective. The intertextuality and unresolved questions at the end of "Supermarket," an early-career poem from 1955, foreshadow Ginsberg's relationship with Whitman in the later volume *Fall of America: Poems of These States 1965-1971*—a relationship characterized by a blend of nostalgia and critique. The poems taken here as case studies for considering the Whitman-Ginsberg interpoetic relationship reveal the ways Ginsberg simultaneously adopts Whitman's topoi and language yet pushes back against a Whitmanian perspective of distant omniscience.

The final line of "Supermarket" bears out an ambivalent perspective on Whitman:

> Ah, dear father, graybeard, lonely old courage-teacher, what America did you have when Charon quit poling his ferry and you got out on a smoking bank and stood watching the boat disappear on the black waters of Lethe? (*Collected* 144)

In its sighing start, this line conjures the diction of "Crossing Brooklyn Ferry": "Ah, what can ever be more stately and admirable to me than mast-hemm'd Manhattan?," the speaker asks at the beginning of Canto 8 (*Leaves* 139). Although the apostrophic ending of "Supermarket" romanticizes the poetic past, the invocation of the classical model ultimately hints at what Ginsberg finds missing from his Whitmanian intertext. By allusively linking Whitman's ferry to Charon's, Whitman's Brooklyn to a "smoking bank," and his harbor to "the black waters of Lethe," Ginsberg criticizes the fact that Whitman leaves dystopian details of his New York surroundings—such as the "the fires from the foundry chimneys burning high and glaringly into the night" in the penultimate line of Canto 3—minimal, sketchy, and latent (*Leaves* 137). James Machor has observed that Whitman's poetic cities are not mimetic;

the city of "Crossing Brooklyn Ferry" is a case in point. Whitman may have had pressing concerns about environmental destruction resulting from the growth of New York City in the 1850s, but as Machor observes, "Whitman can limn his harmonious picture only by ignoring…the problems of industrialization. But those problems are irrelevant to Whitman. He is not writing about social actualities but is composing a poetic world" (182). In other words, what we might call Whitman's poetic machinery—elements such as the poem's patterning of exclamatory and catalogue-type utterances, the self-consciousness of its voice, or the richness of its selected images—prevails over the desire to depict the views from the ferry in a historically accurate fashion. As Whitman aligns the urban and the natural in his poem, he shows a preference for aesthetic conceit rather than realistic representation.

When the speaker of "Supermarket" addresses Whitman at the end of the poem, he is troubled by this allocation of priorities. As his poem asks "What America did you have," Ginsberg implies that in "Crossing Brooklyn Ferry," Whitman has not adequately, convincingly, or personally ("where were *you*?") answered this very question. At the same time as he alludes to Whitman's fascination with the ferry as an allegory for timelessness, Ginsberg rejects one of the fundamental premises of his Whitmanian intertext: that the poet can comment as an omnipotent voice outside time. In "Supermarket," Ginsberg presses Whitman to honor more specifically the declaration in "Crossing"—"I stop here to-day and to-night" (*Leaves* 137)—and presses him into being more forthright about the potentially omitted details. In "Crossing," the "fires from the foundry chimneys burning high and glaringly into the night" (137) and the later "dark patches" (138) are present but abstract, tempered by the imagined harmony between the natural and the urban and by the speaker's reassuring omniscience. By contrast, there is no escaping the burning earth and toxic river in "Supermarket," whose speaker forces the "lonely old" Whitman to be more than a floating, universal presence who remains conveniently free from addressing the realities of his earthly transactions. In the new context, the Whitman figure must stop, get out of the vessel, and watch the boat disappear. Ginsberg's creative manipulation thus subtly reveals the poet he wishes Whitman could be: more stringent in his comments on the unattractive features of urban modernity, more expressive of the particulars of human transience.

Such ambivalence about Whitman more fully saturates the later volume *The Fall of America: Poems of These States 1965-1971*. Ginsberg's nostalgic engagement with Whitman is just as explicit as in "Supermarket" as he dedicates the volume to Whitman and frames it with the following epigraph from the latter's *Democratic Vistas*:

GINSBERG'S AMBIVALENT WHITMAN   *Rounds*

> *Intense and loving comradeship, the personal and passionate attachment of man to man—which, hard to define, underlies the lesson and ideals of the profound saviors of every land and age, and which seems to promise, when thoroughly develop'd, cultivated and recognized in manners and literature, the most substantial hope and safety of the future of these States, will then be fully express'd.*
>
> *It is to the development, identification, and general prevalence of that fervid comradeship, (the adhesive love, at least rivaling the amative love hitherto possessing imaginative literature, if not going beyond it,) that I look for the counterbalance and offset of our materialistic and vulgar American democracy, and for the spiritualization thereof. Many will say it is a dream, and will not follow my inferences; but I confidently expect a time when there will be seen, running like a half-hid warp through all the myriad audible and visible worldly interests of America, threads of manly friendship, fond and loving, pure and sweet, strong and life-long, carried to degrees hitherto unknown—not only giving tone to individual character, and making it unprecedentedly emotional, muscular, heroic, and refined, but having the deepest relations to general politics. I say democracy infers such loving comradeship, as its most inevitable twin or counterpart, without which it will be incomplete, in vain, and incapable of perpetuating itself.* —Democratic Vistas, 1871 (*Fall*, front matter)

Ginsberg looks back at Whitman here, taking care to include the date of composition with the title in the attribution, and the epigraph acts as a way for him to reminiscence about the America of Whitman's imagination. Taken with the nod to Whitman in the book's concluding "After Words" section ("Texts here dedicated to Whitman Good Grey Poet"), the epigraph implies Ginsberg's shared faith in the power of "intense and loving comradeship" and "adhesive love." Beyond the epigraph, the poems in *The Fall of America* are marked by Whitmanian moves. Whitman had a fondness for participles, the part of speech that allowed him, as Ezra Greenspan has described, to "realize his kinetic vision of...'sprawl'—of life as ceaseless, unauthorized (except as self-authorized) motion; of experience as an ongoing process" (96). This favorite Whitmanian part of speech also prevails among Ginsberg's titles in *The Fall of America*—"Beginning a Poem of These States"; "Bayonne Entering NYC"; "Returning North of Vortex," "Smoke Rolling Down Street," "Rising Over Night-Blackened Detroit Streets"—as well as within individual poems. Ginsberg's long lines echo Whitman, as does his manipulation of word order for dramatic effect, as when, in "Beginning a Poem of These States," he withholds the crucial element of a clause until its end: "All memory at once present time returning" (*Fall* 4). Phrases such as "these states," whose provenance Ginsberg reveals in the *Democratic Vistas* epigraph, or the use in "Bayonne Entering NYC" and "After

Words" of one of Whitman's preferred monikers for New York, "Mannahatta," demonstrate Ginsberg's fluency in and fondness for Whitmanian diction.

Yet each of these choices holds as much tension as it does nostalgia. The *Democratic Vistas* epigraph is also an interrogation of Whitman's optimism, a critique of utopian sensibility: as Ginsberg uses Whitman's words as a frame for what he explicitly titles a "fall," Ginsberg imbues Whitman with irony, suggesting that his (Ginsberg's) own later poems are proof that this dream has gone unfulfilled. Within individual poems, Ginsberg deploys Whitmanian vocabulary, syntax, and celebratory kinetic perspective but integrates these elements into vivid and critical portrayals of contemporary American land- and cityscapes. Lines from the middle of the travelogue poem, "Bayonne Entering NYC," exemplify this sort of integration:

>   Light parade everywhere
>   *Motel Hotel*
>   *Lincoln Tunnel*
>   *Pittsburg Shitsburg*
>   *Seagram's a Sure One*
>   Macdaniels vast parkinglot —
>   Cliff rooms, balconies & giant nineteenth
>   century schools,
>   reptilian trucks on Jersey roads
> Manhattan star-spread behind Ft. Lee cliffside
>   Evening lights reflected across Hudson water —
>   brilliant diamond-lantern'd Tunnel
>   Whizz of bus-trucks shimmer in Ear
>   over red brick
>   under Whitmanic Yawp Harbor here
>   roll into Man city, my city, Mannahatta
>   Lower East Side ghosted &
>   grimed with heroin, shit-black from Edison towers
>   on East River's rib — (*Fall* 37)

The Whitman of "Song of Myself" is present in Ginsberg's allusion to the "Yawp Harbor," the Whitman of "Crossing Brooklyn Ferry" present in the position of the river crossing Ginsberg adopts, as well as in his claim on the city of Manhattan and its environs—a claim Whitman makes in Canto 5 of "Crossing": "I too lived, Brooklyn of ample hills was mine, / I too walk'd the streets of Manhattan island, and bathed in the waters around it" (*Leaves* 137). Whitman is woven both into the speaker's vocabulary and professed activities in the poem.

The "Bayonne" poem resembles "Crossing Brooklyn Ferry" in another important respect as well. In "Crossing," vision is Whitman's predominant mode of sensation: "I see you also face to face," the speaker declares to the tide, the clouds, and the sun in the opening section of the poem. For Whitman in this poem, looking becomes the basis of mutually productive communication: "Others... look back on me, because I look'd forward to them" (*Leaves* 137). Even when the gaze is not mutual, it is still the source of pleasure: "Who knows but I am enjoying this? / Who knows, for all the distance, but I am as good as looking at you know, for all you cannot see me?" (*Leaves* 139). Lines such as these hint at what the glance in a crowd of New Yorkers did for Whitman: in Philip Lopate's candid phrasing, "It turned him on. His gaze peeled beneath the city's houses to the ghosts of remembered or fantasized erotic encounters. The crowd was for him a continually tantalizing, pullulating field of sexual potential" (203-4). The gaze and the glance as catalysts for being turned on, in the full possible range of that experience from the erotic to the potentially transhistorical to the imaginary, marks the way Whitman self-presents in his urban poems, "Crossing" in particular. And like the speaker of "Crossing," the speaker of "Bayonne" takes pleasure not only in wondering about or connecting with other city dwellers, but doing so as part of watching and observing them.

Near the end of the poem, Ginsberg remarks, "Gee it's a Miracle to be back on this street / where strange guy mustache / stares in the windowshield" (*Fall* 38). From his car, a position that enables a ghostlike, removed hovering similar to what Whitman enacts in "Crossing," Ginsberg also establishes a visual intimacy with other New Yorkers, seeing, for example, a "Sixth Avenue bus back-window bright glass / Lady in kerchief leans backward, / corner Whalen's drugs, an old Beret familiar face / nods goodbye girl" (*Fall* 39). Ginsberg characterizes these city-dwellers as simultaneously strange and familiar, the equivalent to the men and women who are "curious" to Whitman in "Crossing." "Bayonne" draws attention both to the fact of the speaker's urban sight (a *miracle* to be back on this street) and the corresponding recognition, fantasy, and connection (a *familiar* face) that can occur through this sensory channel.

On the other hand, in a poem such as "Bayonne," Ginsberg is engaging in a mimetic process whose resultant poetics are in stark contrast to Whitman's. Many poems in *The Fall of America* were written while Ginsberg traveled across the United States in a Volkswagen Microbus in 1965. In the "After Words," Ginsberg describes his writing process:

> Beginning with "long poem of these States," *The Fall of America* continues *Planet News* chronicle taperecorded scribed by hand or sung condensed, the flux of car bus airplane dream consciousness Person during Automated Electronic

> War years, newspaper headline radio brain auto poesy & silent desk musings, headlights flashing on road through these States of consciousness. (189)

The direct quotation from road signs in "Bayonne" conveys this unedited effect of a "chronicle taperecorded," a form of sampling Ginsberg highlights typographically through italics and capitalization: "Bayonne refineries behind Newark Hell-light / truck trains passing trans-continental gas lines, / blinking safety signs KEEP AWAKE" (*Fall* 35); "STOP—PAY TOLL" (37); "*Lincoln Tunnel*" (37); "*Seagram's a Sure One* " (72). Other poems integrate song lyrics and radio newscasts in a similarly unfiltered and grammatically unorthodox manner. In "Bayonne," this style of immediacy creates a jarring rift between Ginsberg and Whitman, transposing the latter into a more specific key. "Under Whitmanic Yawp Harbor here / roll into Man city, my city, Mannahatta / Lower East Side ghosted & / grimed with heroin, shit-black": even as Ginsberg draws from Whitman's register, he chooses to juxtapose Whitman's joyous New Yorker persona as signposted by "Yawp" and "Mannahatta" with his own coarser diction describing the Lower East Side. Such rapid transition heightens the sense of difference between the two poets' vocabularies and furthermore creates the impression of contrast between Whitman's world as one of deliberate performative utterance and poesis ("I sound my barbaric yawp over the roofs of the world"), and Ginsberg's world as one of uncensored mimesis. Because of the changes that necessarily occur in the switch between the media of mind, or eye, or ear, and the page, no poem can be an unfiltered transcription of reality. *Pace* recording technology, no poem is completely unstylized. But if we think back to Machor's characterization of Whitman's urban poetics as harmonious, at the (understandable) expense of ignoring some of the social realities from which it stemmed, Ginsberg's mode of urban poetry as exemplified in "Bayonne" seems stylized the other way: linguistically and typographically designed to draw attention to the interruptive, the ugly, the blatantly commercial, and the mundane aspects of passing through built environments.

Echoing such an idea of fundamental difference between Whitman and Ginsberg, Justin Quinn posits that Ginsberg represents a turn in the tradition of the American sublime: "His negotiation between history and spiritual rapture is crucially different from that of the nineteenth century…Ginsberg socializes and 'familiarizes' the sublime: friends, family, and even the larger patterns of national fate are…imbricated within the very texture of his transcendental experience" (194). Pointing to possible common ground, critics such as Lytle Shaw have said that Ginsberg simply "drew out the utopian, unfamiliar, and even contestatory elements of Whitman in order to turn him into a countercultural ally from the 1950s onward…[Ginsberg focuses] in on, and explor[es], tensions already latent in Whitman's celebration of urbanism—his situating of the city at the center of his democratic, corporeal poetics" (79). These two interpretations are not necessarily in conflict, however. In both "Supermarket" and "Bayonne," Ginsberg exposes the underside of "Crossing Brooklyn Ferry," privileging personal and gritty details even as he alludes to a Whitmanian humanistic vision.

"Will we walk all night through solitary streets?" Ginsberg asks his imagined Whitman at the end of "Supermarket." "The trees add shade to shade, lights out in the houses, we'll both be lonely" (*Collected* 144). A subtle ambivalence and teasing tension arise when the notion of "both" and the notion of "lonely" are simultaneously in play; taking at least an initial cue from this early poem, I would suggest that such a pleasingly charged dynamic characterizes the way Ginsberg references Whitman, here and later in his career. We'll both be lonely: in a profound yet unsettled literary relationship that transcends the literal places either of them inhabited and wrote about, these two poets remain together as they come apart.

Works Cited

Ginsberg, Allen. *Collected Poems 1947–1997.* New York: Harper Collins, 2006. Print.

—. *The Fall of America: Poems of These States 1965–1971.* San Francisco: City Lights Books, 1972. Print.

Greenspan, Ezra. "Some Remarks on the Poetics of 'Participle-Loving Whitman.'" *The Cambridge Companion to Walt Whitman.* Ed. Ezra Greenspan. New York: Cambridge UP, 1992. 92-109. Print.

Lopate, Philip. *Waterfront: A Walk Around Manhattan.* New York: Anchor Books/ Random House, 2005. Print.

Machor, James L. *Pastoral Cities: Urban Ideals and the Symbolic Landscape of America.* Madison: U of Wisconsin P, 1987. Print.

Quinn, Justin. "Coteries, Landscape and the Sublime in Allen Ginsberg." *Journal of Modern Literature* 27.1-2 (Fall 2003): 193-206. JSTOR. Web. 3 August 2014.

Shaw, Lytle. "Whitman's Urbanism." *The Cambridge Companion to the Literature of New York.* Ed. Cyrus R. K. Patell and Bryan Waterman. New York: Cambridge UP, 2010. 76-89. Print.

Whitman, Walt. *Leaves of Grass and Other Writings.* Ed. Michael Moon. New York: Norton, 2002. Print.

Gary Snyder, Counterculture, and National Identity
John Whalen-Bridge

> ...*as Paleolithic yogin, must try hunting again—eat venison and acorn bread in the Sierra.*
> —Gary Snyder, *The Selected Letters*

Counterculture and the Outsider's Paradox

"Counterculture" is a widely-used word that covers many circumstances. Christopher Gair usefully opens his study, *The American Counterculture*, by insisting that we must distinguish between myths and histories of this movement, and "that there is a slippery and often uneasy relationship between 'mainstream' and 'marginal'" (2). Rather than draw the lines too firmly when relating the emergent to the mainstream, we should keep in mind that "it is not always possible or desirable to tell the two apart with absolute certainty" (2). And—one last caveat—it would also be a mistake to see the postwar counterculture as monolithic in its resistance to mainstream values. Gair quotes Alice Echols, who, contrary to the typical belief that counterculture went too far in its libertinism, argues that "the hippie subculture mirrored the values of the dominant culture, especially in regard to gays and women" (qtd. in Gair 9).

In addition to continuities and contradictions, there is the primary conundrum of countercultural expression: success is failure. Counterculture can refer to an alternative system of values that means to supplant values understood to be mainstream, but the dissenting voices that became nationally prominent were in danger of being seen as part of the culture industry. To engage too directly with what is mainstream, for example by publishing in highly prominent venues, is to bring into question the author's status as an "outsider." One way of resolving this problem would be to conceive of the countercultural stance as a mere rhetorical gesture, an exaggerated presentation of oneself as alien-to-a-system, when it may later come to seem that "alienation" and "rebellion" were in fact advantageous ways of spinning the fact that that artist has not yet earned as much professional stature (meaning esteem by serving as gatekeepers, being included in anthologies, receiving academic attention, and so forth) as more established writers. Looked at in this way, the countercultural stance can be reduced to nothing more than a self-serving pose, but that is not the purpose of the present enquiry. Rather, it is presumed that the artist wants to be artistically successful (and to be rewarded for their hard work in terms of commercial success) while at the same time developing as a countercultural activist within the domain of literary creation. To this end, it is useful to consider the different ways writers have constructed their opposition to what they, in their imaginative work and in non-fictional or propositional statements, construct as "mainstream." Gary Snyder's always-careful phrasing about national identity is instructive in this consideration, as he resists saying "America" in a habitual way that would tend to concretize the national borders and personal identifications that are reified—made to seem self-evident, normal, natural, and perhaps even ineluctable—by the educational practices and cultural institutions prominent within the United States.

Assuming an artist whose powers grow year by year and book by book, who attracts a following and who becomes a *nationally* recognized creative writer, we find that dilemmas invariably arise about the development of public image, including affiliations that may become apparent within the writing and through biographical acts, and in the writer's developing relationship to a growing audience. Commercial success, then, can be construed as a threat to authenticity, since dissident voices can be commodified and assimilated in various ways either at the level of composition or reception. Postwar American culture has been particularly resilient in the face of countercultural critique, co-opting acts of rebellion and revolutionary proclamations. An image, style, or theme that is associated with serious challenges to a social order can develop into differences of lifestyle and taste that are in reality not a challenge to a system of social organization. The image of Che Guevara can be used to sell shirts, and, as suggested, Romantic writer rebellion can be a strategy for becoming a "great American writer." Consider Alfred Kazin's thoughts about Norman Mailer in 1980, perhaps at the height of his reputation as a novelist, in Kazin's comments about *The Executioner's Song*. Kazin has grown weary of Mailer's celebration of the "psychic outlaw" notion that Mailer developed in his 1957 manifesto "The White Negro," and Kazin thinks Mailer's literature has become a self-serving pose: "Mailer thinks he's a great rebel. But I believe that if I reviewed the whole postwar history, I'd find that he's riding the waves exactly like a surfboard. It's fashion and show biz" (Manso 650).[1]

We construe from various reference points a countercultural identity, usually in relation to a "movement" of some sort, sometimes forgetting the variety of motivations contributing to the reified entity collected by a given name. Theodore Roszak reviews this problem carefully in *The Making of a Counter Culture* (1969), drawing our attention to the gaps between broad gestures and the implicit social consequences they would appear to contain:

> If Allen Ginsberg's *Howl* stands as a founding document of the counter culture, we must remember that the poet had to tell the world: "I have burned all my money in a waste-basket." Will it be a victory, then, or a defeat for the counter culture when the black man has at last fought his way clear of desperate expedients and wrings from the Great Society the white man's legal equivalent of looting: a steady job, a secure income, easy credit, free access to all the local emporiums, and his own home to pile the merchandise in? (67)

Come again? Let us assume that Roszak knows the difference between poetic flights of fancy and prosaic precision and that he chooses the image of the poet burning his money to question the relationship between poetic provocations, on the one hand, and the meaning of political opposition on the other. The question becomes, "Is the poet for reform or revolution?" Is the poetry of counterculture using poetic connotations and provocative incitements to move us toward the abolition of a corrupt way of life, or is all of the shouting a nudge in the direction of social amelioration? There is a contradiction of sorts between the angry rejection of a way of life within the angry verse and the wish—perhaps nourished by the poem, but perhaps not—that America is fixable. Johnson's Great Society was a plan for fixing America, and if one is for it, then one is "for" mainstream American society. One's credentials as a counterculturalist, then, can be endangered if the work is associated with direct social improvement. When revolutionary rhetoric garners authenticity by attacking the falsehood of mainstream society, it is haunted in this way by the specter of reform.

Roszak develops the point about counterculture in relation to racial injustice. It would not be a loss in terms of the claimed values of Beats, New Left activists, Hippies, and so forth for racism to decline and for equal opportunity to increase, but the symbolic action of countercultural activity, including the creation of poetry such as "Howl" and numerous other Beat manifestos, also involves the celebration of a space outside the mainstream. The imagined subject position both affirms its own right to exist just as it complains that its causal condition—some unfairness or injustice in "the system"—ought to be rectified. Roszak writes,

> What, after all, does social justice mean to the outcast and the dispossessed? Most obviously it means gain in admission to everything from which middleclass selfishness excludes them. But how does one achieve such admission without simultaneously becoming an integral and supportive element of the technocracy? (68)

A counterculture exists when a group forms around norms and values that are markedly at odds with those of the so-called mainstream, by which I mean the plurality of possible values and norms that differ from one another in various ways but which nonetheless appear within the system of a given identity rather than outside of it. My simple point is that Gary Snyder's always-careful iteration of "America" or "the United States" develops ways of thinking about contemporary American culture that can refer to it knowledgably while still retaining a space that is outside of it. The literary and social practices he has developed since appearing within the American public imagination in the mid-1950s are not merely different by degrees. Although Snyder frequently describes ways of inhabiting the world in a sustainable rather than exploitative way, he does not place all his hopes in the possibility that "America" will change course to become the kind of social order of which he could fully approve. Readers who identify with Snyder's social vision are encouraged by his vision of a post-American future—a return to Turtle Island.

Impermanence as Hope: Outlasting America

I wish to consider Snyder's countercultural thought in relation to the way he refers to "the United States of America"—or rather in relation to the way he avoids hailing into existence "Americans" as much as possible. In the early and middle parts of his career, it is as if America is the nation that shall not be named, and he displaces reference to it, for example by calling it "Turtle Island."[2] Or, he boycotts reference to *national* borders, preferring to enshrine in poems bioregional markers that, in his work, trump national identity. Occasionally he squares off against "America," which is usually a sign to designate the most concentrated assortment of symptoms of empire more broadly called "the West." The title of this essay might seem to suggest that all countercultural writers work from a similar standpoint, but Snyder stands apart. He has moments of affection for "America," particularly for a quality of open-heartedness that he is willing to associate with "America" rather than just California or a bioregional designation, but for the most part his value structure diminishes the significance of attempts to fix America or mourn its failings within the scope of a generation or a lifetime. Rather, Snyder means to wait out the nation-state, which means thinking in a more-than-my-lifetime way. Synthesizing elements drawn from Buddhism and archaic social systems, Snyder foresees a more sustainable "planetary culture," by which he means

> the kind of society that would follow on a new understanding of that relatively recent institution, the National State, an understanding that might enable us to leave it behind. The State is greed made legal, with a monopoly

> on violence; a natural society is familial and cautionary. A natural society is one that "Follows the Way," imperfectly but authentically.³ (*Reader* 43)

Snyder throws down a gauntlet of sorts, calling out the urban/national ideologies that go largely unquestioned by the mainstream readerships and literary gatekeepers who have considerable power in shaping literary and artistic cultural trends. Yet his design is not to take arms against this sea of troubles but, rather, to survive it. Put another way, the Snyder of *Earth House Hold* imagines a future in which the fossil fuels run out, and a smaller population of humans will return—happily, in Snyder's prophetic imaginings—to a life that is tribal and bioregional. The case of Snyder throws what we nominalize as a monolithic counterculture into relief and allows us to see significant differences between leftist-progressive writers such as the Beats and their various literary cousins.

Michael McClure has paid homage to Kenneth Rexroth as the intellectual impresario who gathered countercultural impulses into a movement (42). Rexroth, however, in a 1970 essay that takes swipes at the "senile establishment" which was celebrating Paul Goodman as the resident renegade, singles out Snyder as the chief ideologue of the emerging counterculture. How odd to see the word "ideologist" used as a compliment here:

> Gary Snyder is unquestionably the leading ideologist and critic of the counter-culture, but he is that, not discursively, but as a poet whose values are exposed in the factual experience of the poem with the presentational immediacy of concrete happenings. The ideology is the perspective. The criticism is in the arrangement. The dead culture is challenged not by rhetorical judgment but by assimilable occurrences. (Rexroth, n.pag.)

In his critical prose, Rexroth jumps from one brilliant *apercu* to the next, and it is worthwhile to unpack his discourse. "Assimilation" can be either a very good thing or a sign that oppositional approaches to mainstream, hegemonic lifeways will not succeed. In the sentence just quoted, Snyder is not an ideologist in the sense that he abstracts himself from the social process and writes highly intellectual essays that make evident his elevation above the hoi polloi. Rexroth praises the poetry that leads and teaches not by appointing itself an intellectual dictatorship of the proletarian sub-poets. Rather, Snyder's work succeeds best when it directly and with apparent simplicity apprehends an experience in a manner that invites similar apprehension from a reader, perhaps creating an aesthetic effect that momentarily elides the subject/object divisions between self and subject matter, or between reader and audience. Snyder, as we have seen, draws on both Buddhadharma and celebratory notions of the primitive as guiding values for a society that "follows the way" (*Reader* 43), and in line with these stated ideals he has developed a poetics and a poetic praxis that very much encourage an understanding of the supposed other as a continuation or reflection of some aspect of the self. It is a democratic breakthrough in which the heightened perception of the poet is shared as widely as possible.

Rexroth worries that the revolutionary ambitions of a poetry and broader cultural movement intent on promoting a genuinely alternative way of life is endangered by the power of contemporary American life to co-opt apparent threats. Bad assimilation occurs for Rexroth when a supposedly countercultural writer makes the mainstream audience "uncomfortable" in a way that is actually flattering—the reader who is chided by a slightly more radical writer is also given attention, and this is flattering. Honestly, we like it when the poet attacks our society (though we may fantasize ourselves as the exception to the jeremiad), as such critiques undoubtedly unify a "we" and give that selfhood a spotlight in which to shine. With these worries in mind, mama-bear Rexroth gives Ginsberg a pedagogical paw-slap:

> Allen Ginsberg is assimilable. We can always make room in the canon for Hosea. The prophet, the *nabi*, is a standard appurtenance of the Solomonic court. Ginsberg must struggle continuously to keep from being digested. Even so he is one of America's Hundred Best Celebrities. (n.pag.)

I *think* this statement was a compliment, but it is certainly a back-handed one. Ginsberg, in Rexroth's figuration, is in between fates. It is possible that he will not demand a radical change in the social order, since he would not be thusly embraced if he were. Or, he may "struggle continuously to keep from being digested." Therein lies the inherent drama of countercultural resistance, which makes it distinct from revolutionary resistance on the one hand and liberal reform on the other. Of course, one can be in favor of liberal reform in the short run while planning a wholly different way of life in the long run (or at least we used to think so before the term "Anthropocene" became normal). While allowing for the possibility that Ginsberg would continue to resist co-optation, Rexroth notes a possible weakness in Ginsberg's way of relating to American society, namely that the gadfly who is apparently against the social structure is easily accommodated by that structure. Calling Ginsberg "one of America's Hundred Best Celebrities" is to a lesser degree a nod to the younger poet's relative value in popularizing countercultural sentiments, but a word like "Celebrities" suggests inconsequential glamor more than anything else. The capital letters imitate and mock the puffed-up world in which prominence exists without the sort of achievements Rexroth would rather recognize.

Snyder has written a series of essays and longer prose statements calling for specific changes in attitude and behavior (e.g., "Four Changes," *Reader* 245-53). The Rexroth assertion that this writer known primarily for his poetry is nonetheless an important "ideologist" of the counterculture is a direction to his readers as to where safe counsel about how to avoid co-optation can be found. One thing that makes Snyder different from postwar prophetic critics such as Mailer and Ginsberg is that Snyder rarely performs the "love/hate relationship" with America, in which the national identity would be just fine if American institutions and other social forces and groups would live up to the values stated in the Declaration of Independence, and so forth. For Snyder, national identity is a bad habit we will be stuck with until enough people experience a philosophical shift toward anarchistic self-organization, a shift that entails a bioregional understanding of the landscape. Snyder often reminds readers that the right angles and parallel lines on American maps—think of Four Corners, the spot on the map where Colorado, New Mexico, Arizona, and Nevada meet—measure the colonial domination of "Turtle Island," the name for North America that originates in First Nation mythic origin stories in which the world rests on a turtle's back. This usage does not therefore repress indigenous ways of conceiving of North American place and space, although Snyder does occasionally refer to America and, of course, he addresses American readers.

There is a certain intimacy when Ginsberg says, "Go fuck yourself with your atom bomb." It is the direct harshness that is possible in a family fight. Snyder too exhibits something of a love/hate relationship with America in his work of the sixties and seventies, but it is never quite like Ginsberg's prophetic call to account. He is briefly tempted to love America but gives the personified self the cold shoulder in poems such as "I Went into a Maverick Bar," announcing that he can *almost* love America at its most blue-collar, but not quite. In poem after poem, America is the negative backdrop, the foil, to a discussion of a virtuous East Asian or pre-industrial-revolution community. In various satires and diatribes, the word *America* is more or less spat out or is voiced in a thoroughly condescending way, such as in these lines from "Maverick Bar":

> They held each other like in High School dances
>   in the fifties;
> I recalled when I worked in the woods
>   and the bars of Madras, Oregon.
> That short-haired joy and roughness—
>   America—your stupidity.
> I could almost love you again. (*Turtle Island* 9)

Contrast this with Ginsberg's full-throated family-fight with America (entitled "America"), a rant that very much wants to redeem an America that fails to live up to its own potential:

> America I've given you all and now I'm nothing.
> America two dollars and twenty-seven cents January 17, 1956.
> I can't stand my own mind.
> America when will we end the human war?
> Go fuck yourself with your atom bomb
> I don't feel good don't bother me.
> I won't write my poem till I'm in my right mind.
> America when will you be angelic? (62)

The flaws of the self often mirror the failings of the nation, and so, in Whitmanian manner, the poet often marries himself to the nation for better or for worse. Ginsberg, like Rexroth, is angry with America, but he holds out the possibility that American will be "angelic" in a way we would not expect from Rexroth. Snyder consistently avoids an America-centric world-view, just as he created his own 40,000-year dating system to avoid using the Common Era (CE) system based on the life of Christ. He addresses the reality of the nation state, but this is often a necessary compromise in an attempt to induce a shift in standpoint and in identification among his readers. Reform would be welcome but unlikely; those who see the light will instead prepare the way for the bioregional, sustainable communities of the post-petroleum future.

Snyder came to his wilderness-oriented system of values early, and it remains in late works such as *Mountains and Rivers Without End, Danger on Peaks*, and the essay collection *Back on Fire*. His primary orientation has not changed: rather than be "assimilated" by America, he holds his ground and waits for America, or whatever it will call itself, to come around. As he had presented his view in his 1960s writings, his position is carved in stone—paleolithic stone:

> As a poet I hold the most archaic values on earth. They go back to the upper Paleolithic: the fertility of the soil, the magic of animals, the power-vision in solitude, the terrifying initiation and rebirth, the love and ecstasy of the dance, the common work of the tribe. (*Myths and Texts* viii)

His army does not directly engage with such enemies as the neo-liberal state in a take-arms-against-a-sea-of-troubles way, though he does speak truth back to the power of urban ideology, a hegemonic discourse that has defined and reified a sense of "wilderness" and "nature" in ways that powerfully condition thinking.

SNYDER AND NATIONAL IDENTITY Whalen-Bridge

As an ideologist, Snyder directly challenges the legitimacy of habitual language, drawing out the histories and etymologies of key words that subtly and mostly unconsciously shape the pathways of thought. In line with his general critique of anthropomorphic imagination and the way in which people measure life according to what they imagine their own lifespan will be, he would rather think in terms of centuries or chunks of time on the order of 50,000 years, an idea he works out in his essay "Entering the Fiftieth Millennium" (*Back on Fire* 73-79). In a manner that harkens back to Robinson Jeffers's "inhumanism," Snyder nudges readers beyond the humanist scale of time that focuses on the next twenty or fifty years—a period that will directly affect us and our children. Sometimes, when absolutely necessary, Snyder will engage in what might be construed as an imaginary conversation with the nation state, but when he does, it is to attempt to bring the nation state around to his way of thinking. For example, in his essay "Thinking Toward the Thousand-Year Forest Plan," he acknowledges that many people in America will not typically imagine their responsibilities toward the future in thousand-year terms, but he counters that the American government does precisely this when forced to by circumstances:

> Someday there will be a Thousand-year Forest Plan. If talking about "one thousand years" seems unimaginably long, we should remember that the Department of Energy and the whole nuclear establishment are planning for a repository of spent but thoroughly dangerous radioactive material to be placed underground at Yucca Mountain in Nevada, and it will need to be overseen and guarded for at least ten thousand years. They have assured us that they will look after it for all that time. (*Back on Fire* 40)

Snyder does not have complete confidence, to say the least, that nation states will last the ten thousand years necessary to fulfill such a promise. In *Mountains and Rivers Without End* and *Danger on Peaks*, his major poetry collections from 1996 and 2004, respectively, he is increasingly concerned with transience, mortality, and the need to recognize the temporal rhythms of existence. A breath is just a breath, and a national language might have a 500-year life span. But attending to the rhythms of mortality also allows for patterns of renewal. In "Covers the Ground" from *Mountains and Rivers Without End*, he sings of the California that existed maybe 400 years ago:

> *"The Great Central Plain of California*
> *was one smooth bed of honey-bloom*
> *   400 miles, your foot would press*
> *a hundred flowers at every step*

> *it seemed one sheet of plant gold;*
>
> *all the ground was covered*
> *with radiant corollas ankle-deep. . . ."* (68, Snyder's italics)

This passage, carved from John Muir's writing about the Sierras, is not only about what once *was*; in Snyder's vision, it can be *again*.[4]

In the meantime, the current world of America is characterized by severe addiction: "Once a bear gets hooked on garbage there's no cure" (*The Back Country* 76), and it is hard to overcome the lazy thrill of cheap energy-addiction for man and bear alike. That said, Snyder hopes the junk will run out, the damage to the ecosystem done during the "homocene" will be as little as possible, and then life without monoculture will continue and thrive. Unlike other countercultural visionaries, Snyder is not a "humanist," if that word means that one measures the value of all things in terms of a human life, unconsciously assuming an urban, intellectual, semi-elite life, at that. In Robinson Jeffers's sense of the term, he is an "inhumanist," although he attempts to shake off the Schopenhauerian superior glare of Jeffers. Snyder's imagination of our possible wide-scale return to reinhabitory relations with the ground beneath us and life forms around us is as open-hearted and light-spirited as he can make it, given the merciless encroachment of industrial life and urban ideology on all other lifeways.

The final poem of *Mountains and Rivers* is entitled "Finding a Space in the Heart," and it has a prophetic dimension (in Cornel West's sense of the term), which involves being a moral witness and aligning with a right way of living. The poem recounts several moments when Snyder saw "it," which I take to mean a vision of the world and self as non-separate. The poem begins,

> I first saw it in the sixties,
> driving, a Volkswagon camper
> with a fierce gay poet and a
> lovely but dangerous girl with a husky voice.... (*Mountains* 149)

What did he see? "Mountains, lava flow caves, / the Alvord desert—pronghorn ranges— / and the glittering obsidian-paved / dirt track toward Vya" (149). What we see so far are signifiers connected to a particular progressive-liberal way of life, vast spaces defined by animals of various sorts and not just humans, and a landscape that opens up into the open-endedness that is referred to in Buddhist religious and philosophical texts as emptiness. In a moment of ecstasy, the poet describes the part that cannot completely be fenced in by words: "*O, ah! The / awareness of emptiness / brings forth a heart of compassion!*" (149). Emptiness

SNYDER AND NATIONAL IDENTITY Whalen-Bridge

is intrinsically related to impermanence but contains the nuances of freedom from deterministic shackles—empty of constraint, we might say—as well as the emptiness of permanent selfhood.

Our bodies certainly lack permanent, stable selfhood: they all fall apart as the decades accumulate. We hear a note or so of this sense of loss a few lines later, when the poet writes about the continuation of the Volkswagon journey: "The next day we reached San Francisco / in a time when it seemed / the world might head a new way" (149). Snyder participated in Be-Ins and wrote with great hope, but the hope that the counterculture would change America did not pan out: "it seemed / the world might head a new way." Prospects arise, fall, and give way to retrospective considerations that, in turn, reincarnate in surprising ways: "Fifteen years passed. In the eighties / With my lover I went where the roads end. . . / discovered a path / of carved stone inscriptions tucked into the sagebrush / "Stomp out greed" / "The best things in life are not things." Snyder caps these carved English-language mantras by saying, "words placed by an old desert sage" (150). These messages, carved in rocks, are meant for the future. They are hidden treasures for a future that will resemble the Paleolithic past. The poet then sings of the great inland lakes that have dried up: "cutthroat trout spirit in silt" that will return. After a section that strongly echoes the *via negativa* of the Prajna Paramita Sutra—e.g., no nose, no eye—Snyder closes with a picnic in which one item on the menu is grasshoppers, and the poet looks forward, through the present event in the 1990s, to the possible future when "Americans" go away and the people that remain become neo-native Americans, or something like that.

In *The Practice of the Wild*, Snyder reports that he heard a Crow elder say,

> You know, I think if people stay somewhere long enough—even white people—the spirits will begin to speak to them. It's the power of the spirits coming up from the land. The spirits and the old powers aren't lost, they just need people to be around long enough and the spirits will begin to influence them. (42)

The current moment at the end of *Mountains and Rivers* that anticipates this possible future is not Jeffers-dour but rather Snyder-humorous, when people eat the grasshoppers but not without some resistance:

> and tasting grasshoppers roasted in a pan
>
> > They all somehow swarm down here—
> > sons and daughters in a circle
> > eating grasshoppers grimacing,

> singing sutras for the insects in the wilderness,
>
> —the wideness, the
> Foolish loving spaces
>
> full of heart. (152)

It is important to note that Snyder praises and appreciates actual experiences. The fantasy of a Turtle Island made up of people who co-exist respectfully with the environment is not *merely* a fantasy. By anchoring his vision of community in memories of what has actually occurred—both in the playful experiment with insect-eating, and in the opening poem that shows us the mountains and rivers of T'ang-era China—Snyder proleptically answers the criticism that his vision is utopian. It can happen because it has happened and it does happen.

All identities are provisional and temporary, and the acceptance of impermanence conditions the countercultural affiliations that run through Snyder's work. To identify oneself primarily in countercultural terms is to define oneself forever in opposition, a mistake Snyder certainly avoids in his conclusion to *Mountains and Rivers Without End*. The eaters of grasshoppers grimace, the sutras are sung, and the poet plays with alliteration: it is play that is stressed, not opposition or any kind of agonistic self-fashioning. The readers in early-twenty-first-century America may also grimace about the grasshoppers—we are compelled to identify with a future we cannot fully understand. The community within the poem and the poem's readers are certain, however, to share one quality, and that is the playful (rather than fraught) encounter of impermanence and blissful presence. The sixties came and went, and the children will come and go. In between, there are roasted grasshoppers and the possibility of *appreciating* "insects in the wilderness."

Notes

I would especially like to thank Ronna Johnson and Nancy Grace for their encouragement and sharp editorial eyes.

[1] Kazin, in his comments to interviewer Peter Manso, was expressing anger at Mailer for romanticizing murderers such as Jack Henry Abbott and Gary Gilmore, the central figure of *The Executioner's Song*. In 1968, Mailer wrote an especially celebratory review of Mailer's *Armies of the Night*, a "nonfiction novel" that narrates a symbolic and modestly physical struggle between countercultural forces (e.g., groups organized by yippie figures such as Abbie

Hoffman) and National Guard troops and, symbolically, the Pentagon itself. (1-2, 26).

[2] In addition to Snyder's 1974 book, *Turtle Island*, which won the 1975 Pulitzer Prize for poetry, see especially the essay "Rediscovering Turtle Island" in *A Place in Space*, 236-51.

[3] "Buddhism and the Coming Revolution" was originally published in *Earth House Hold* in 1969, and sections of it are included in *The Gary Snyder Reader*.

[4] Snyder has whittled down three passages by John Muir's "Bee Pastures" chapter from *My First Summer in the Sierras* to form these verses. The Muir passages are as follow, with the words Snyder has "sampled" in italics:

> *The Great Central Plain of California*, during the months of March, April, and May, *was one smooth*, continuous *bed of honey-bloom*, so marvelously rich that, in walking from one end of it to the other, a distance of more than *400 miles, your foot would press* about *a hundred flowers at every step*. (523)

> When I first saw this central garden, the most extensive and regular of all the bee-pastures of the State, *it seemed all one sheet of plant gold*, hazy and vanishing in the distance, distinct as a new map along the foot-hills at my feet. (524)

> Descending the eastern slopes of the Coast Range through beds of gilias and lupines, and around many a breezy hillock and bush-crowned headland, I at length waded out into the midst of it. *All the ground was covered*, not with grass and green leaves, but *with radiant corollas, about ankle-deep* next the foot-hills... (524)

See *John Muir: Nature Writings*.

Works Cited

Gair, Christopher. *The American Counterculture*. Edinburgh: Edinburgh UP, 2007. Print.

Ginsberg Allen and Gary Snyder. *The Selected Letters of Allen Ginsberg and Gary Snyder*. Edited by Bill Morgan. Berkeley, CA: Counterpoint, 2009. Print.

Kazin, Alfred. "The Trouble He's Seen" in *The New York Times* (May 5, 1968: 1-2, 26). Web. 5 Feb. 2016.

Manso, Peter. *Mailer: His Life and Times*. New York: Washington Square, 2008. Print.

McClure, Michael. "Ninety-one Things about Richard Brautigan." *Lighting the Corners: On Art, Nature, and the Visionary*. Albuquerque: U of New Mexico P, 1993. 36-68. Print.

Muir, John. *John Muir: Nature Writings*. Edited by William Cronon. New York: Library of America, 1997. Print.

Rexroth, Kenneth. "Gary Snyder: Smokey the Bear Bodhisattva." Web. n.p., 21 May 2014.

Roszak, Theodore. *The Making of a Counter Culture: Reflections on the Technocratic Society and Its Youthful Opposition*. Berkeley, CA: U of California P, 1968, revised edition 1995. Print.

Snyder, Gary. *A Place in Space: Ethics, Aesthetics, and Watersheds*. Washington, D.C.: Counterpoint, 1995. Print.

—. *The Back Country*. Norfolk, CT: New Directions, 1968. Print.

—. *Back on Fire: Essays*. Washington, DC: Shoemaker & Hoard, 2007. Print.

—. *Danger on Peaks*. Washington, DC: Shoemaker & Hoard, 2004. Print.

—. *The Gary Snyder Reader: Prose, Poetry, and Translations,* 1952-1998. Washington, DC: Counterpoint, 1999. Print.

—. "I Went Into a Maverick Bar." Poetry Foundation. Web. 5 March, 2016.

—. *Mountains and Rivers Without End*. Washington, DC: Counterpoint, 1996. Print.

—. *Myths and Texts*. New York: New Directions, [1960] 1978. Print.

—. *Practice of the Wild*. New York, NY: North Point P, 1990. Print.

—. *Turtle Island*. NY: New Directions. [1969] 1974. Print.

The Beat Interview

Rochelle Owens

Rochelle Owens reading at Kelly Writers House, University of Pennsylvania, Philadelphia, 2013. Photographer: George Economou

INTERVIEW with ROCHELLE OWENS
Amy Friedman

Introduction

The American poet and playwright Rochelle Owens's enduring literary career started with writing trend-setting plays for the nascent Off-Off-Broadway scene in the 1950s and 1960s, and publishing over 18 avant-garde poetry and prose works since 1962. Her publishing continues to the present, with new books and online works. Owens belongs as an innovator in several niches of major American writing since the mid-twentieth century. Her artistic career has seen her name on the bill at poetry readings, in little magazines and anthologies, and featured in theater seasons with a surprising number of Beat Generation writers.

We do not tend to associate Beat Generation writers with experimental theater, but actually many, if not most, Beat Generation artists worked in or had associations with the avant-garde Off-Off-Broadway movement in New York City starting from the late 1950s. Archival theater listings show Judith Malina and Julian Beck of the experimental Living Theatre working with numerous Black Mountain College artists including John Cage and Merce Cunningham, and sponsoring poetry readings at their venue by Jack Kerouac, Allen Ginsberg, and Gregory Corso. Beat poet and City Lights publisher Lawrence Ferlinghetti's play, *The Allegation Impromptu*, written with Tad Mosel, ran at La Mama Theater in New York during the week of March 5, 1964, and was directed by John Parkinson. In the first week of January 1967, poet Jack Micheline, who later settled on the West Coast (and maintained a sometimes vexed relationship with the designation Beat), had his play *East Bleeker* performed at La Mama under the direction of Alex Horn, with music for the show composed by Gary W. Friedman and Frank Wilson. In the same era, Chelsea Theater Center, founded in 1965 by Robert Kalfin, was producing Amiri Baraka's *Slave Ship*, and Allen Ginsberg's already famous poem "Kaddish" was adapted as a stageplay there.

The New York Poets Theatre was founded in early 1961 by Beat poet Diane di Prima, along with her fellow artists, the Beat writer LeRoi Jones (later known as Amiri Baraka), actor Alan Marlowe, writer and choreographer James Waring, dancer Freddie Herko, and musician and composer John Herbert McDowell, in a flurry of buoyant enthusiasm and by extremely modest means. New York Poets Theatre opened its first show that autumn, on October 29, 1961, with a program comprising three pieces, all one notes, by Beat writers: *The Discontent of the Russian Prince*, a play by Diane di Prima, and featuring di Prima and dancer Freddy Herko as the cast; West Coast Beat Poet Michael McClure's verse play *The Pillow*; and LeRoi Jones's drama, *The Eighth Ditch*, from his longer work, *The System of Dante's Hell*.

This confluence of the Beat aesthetic and avant-garde or fringe theater productions will no doubt continue to attract scholarly attention, as this focus gives such a strong purview of the breadth of an individual's oeuvre and a clearer sense of an intertwined artistic community. Rochelle Owens's fundamental view of the avant-garde has always been that it is the product of many modes of artistic practice and diverse expression. My interview with Owens aims to shed some light on that vibrant and influential community as well as on her role as a nonchalantly rule-breaking and ground-breaking artist. The following brief biography helps to place her in the context of avant-garde and Beat writing.

Biography

Rochelle Bass Owens was born April 2, 1936, in Brooklyn, New York. She was drawn to art at an early age, studying ballet for an intense period and relentlessly churning out playscriptsand poems. In her late teens, Owens approached Allen Ginsberg for comments on her poetry; Ginsberg referred her to LeRoi Jones, who was an enthusiastic early supporter and publisher of Owens's work. Owens's meetings in Greenwich Village with LeRoi Jones sparked a warm, enduring friendship with Jones's wife and co-publisher, Hettie Jones. Owens's path through the New York bohemia of jazz cafes, coffee houses, and gatherings in downtown walk ups crossed that of Diane di Prima, who was herself getting started as a poet. In later poetry readings, Owens has shared the bill with Gregory Corso, Allen Ginsberg, Jackson Mac Low, Ed Sanders, and Anne Waldman.

The young Owens was also writing for the stage in a bold manner that reshaped mid-century notions of what was acceptable, objectionable, or obscene in stage performances. By her mid-20s, she had seen Off-Off-Broadway productions of her early works *Homos, Istanboul,* and *The String Game* in small theaters. But the game-changer was Owens's remarkable play *Futz,* which she wrote in 1958 at the age of 23, and which finally premiered at La MaMa Experimental Theatre Club on March 2, 1967, under the stewardship of the legendary avant-garde producer Ellen Stewart. Radical in tone and extremely provocative in subject, this story of a rural

INTERVIEW WITH ROCHELLE OWENS   *Friedman*

pig farmer profoundly enamored of his sow, Amanda, managed simultaneously to stir stern protests and enrapture awards committees. The production was initially banned when it toured to Toronto, since critics decried it as "bestial" and "obscene," and yet in 1967 it won three Obie awards: Best Actor (Seth Allen), Best Director (Tom O'Horgan), and Best Play. Tom O'Horgan would go on to direct the film version of *Futz* in 1969.

In the 1970s, Owens produced book-length works of poetry, including *The Joe 82 Creation Poems* (1974) and *The Joe Chronicles Part 2* (1979). She develops in her longer work an expansive mythos of creation, consistent with her relentless experimentations in a poetic idiom that is highly personal and universal, while simultaneously cryptic and enlightening. Her later career has included lecturing, teaching, composing spoken-word poetry and video-montage works, and more poetry, with no veering from the path of the avant-garde instigator. Controversy followed the on-line publication of her poem "Chomsky Grilling Linguica," at *NewVerseNews* and in the *Golden Handcuffs Review* in 2006. Noam Chomsky supporters railed at the perceived attack on an intellectual icon, while the three-part satiric poem was nominated for two anthologies honoring the best poetry to be published online.

Rochelle Owens is the author of the following: Poetry—*Out of Ur: New & Selected Poems 1961–2012* (Shearsman Books, 2013), *Solitary Workwoman* (Junction Press, 2011), *Triptych* (Texture Press, 2006), *Luca: Discourse on Life and Death* (Junction Press, 2001), *New and Selected Poems 1961–1996* (Junction Press, 1997), *Rubbed Stones* (Texture Press, 1994), *Black Chalk* (Texture Press, 1992), *How Much Paint Does the Painting Need* (Kulchur Foundation, 1988), *W. C. Fields in French Light* (Contact II Publications, 1986), *Constructs* (Point Riders Press, 1985), *The Joe Chronicles Part 2* (Black Sparrow Press, 1979), *Shemuel* (New Rivers Press, 1979), *The Joe 82 Creation Poems* (Black Sparrow Press, 1974), *I Am the Babe of Joseph Stalin's Daughter* (Kulchur Foundation, 1972), *Salt & Core* (Black Sparrow Press, 1968), and *Not Be Essence That Cannot Be* (Trobar Books, 1961); Plays—*Plays by Rochelle Owens* (Broadway Play Publishing, 2000), *Futz and Who Do You Want, Piere Vidal?* (Broadway Play Publishing, 1986), *The Karl Marx Play and Others* (E. P. Dutton & Co., 1974), *Futz and What Came After* (Random House, 1968); and Fiction—*Journey to Purity* (Texture Press, 2009).

Today, the statement we might identify as Owens's overarching mantra can be found in the "Autobiography" section of her current website, *rochelleowens.org:* "Art," Owens contends, "is imbedded in the human spirit."

Interviewer's Note: Rochelle Owens and I spoke during the afternoon of June 11, 2015, at her home in Philadelphia, over tea and cookies. I first explained my provisional structure for our talk: origins, Beats, current work.

Rochelle Owens: So you ask a question...

Amy Friedman: It's quite interesting to start with Jean Genet! How young were you when you came across his work?

RO: I saw a production of *The Balcony* in the West Village. And I think I must have been around 18 or 19, it was at the Circle in the Square Theater, and I thought it was wonderful. Now when you said "origins," does that mean my own beginnings?

AF: I know that's hard to pin down, but I was thinking of giving some sense of how you started as a writer.

RO: In terms of the poetry, at the age of 17, I remember having a job in Manhattan. This was after I graduated high school. I moved to Manhattan at 19, so I was still living in Brooklyn. And I had this job at a sewing machine company that was called Macdowell Associates, where I did the bills of lading for electrical equipment that was for the sewing machines.[1] The plant was in the south, and the office was in Manhattan. And I did the bills of lading, kind of like reception and telephone, and I was expected to do each day's bills of lading. The bills of lading were descriptions of the parts of this equipment, these sewing machines, and the language that was used to describe the equipment was novel for me because they were based on anatomical parts of the body. These were sockets male and female, and they were described, "This is male, this is female," and other technical descriptions, very non-poetic, but they were interesting. I do remember that I was always drawn to something that I could in my mind juxtapose.

My brother is an architect, so that could be a kind of intellectual interest in, where either it's visual or objects, it's words, using unusual, so-called non-poetic language, because remember, this is 1953, '54, '55. My first publication was in, I think, 1958 or '59 in a magazine that came out from California called *Simbolica*, and that was my very first publication.

AF: It was a poem?

RO: Yes, the poem begins "Can I in sin on august green?"[2] I mention it in my autobiography.[3] Charles Bukowski was also published in the same edition of the magazine. I thought the editor was a young man; I was introduced to him by Oscar Williams. Does that name ring a bell?

AF: No.

RO: This is very interesting. In the '40s and '50s, Oscar Williams published every year an anthology of British and American poetry, in hardcover; it was something a young poet would yearn to be included in. It had the authority of the leather-bound edition. I met Oscar Williams, he was much older than me, kind of a wizened old man with glasses. Very of the time, very respectful of the giants of English and American poetry. He wasn't into "The New." He adored Dylan Thomas, well at that time there was a very strong interest in British poetry. But the thing that I remember most was that when we went to the Y on 92nd street, there was Sylvia Plath!

INTERVIEW WITH ROCHELLE OWENS   *Friedman*

AF: Wow.

RO: And I met her. She was very nice. She seemed to have a radiance about her, when you think about her horrible life that she had with Ted Hughes, and she did succeed in saving her two children. She had wound cotton all around the recesses of the doors.

AF: I had read that story, and also been so blown away by *Ariel*, and by her earlier work; she wrote wonderful poetry. The thing that bothers me is that I am not sure that she ever knew it.

RO: I frankly didn't read that much of her poetry. Although her famous one, "Daddy," was certainly interesting. I was very intrigued later on about how horrible her life was. And I met her and she was very friendly. And Oscar Williams was there at the 92nd Street Y, and he talked to an editor in California who was very interested in my work, and I thought this editor, who would go on to publish my work, was my age. It turned out then he was probably in his early 80s. That was amusing! His name was Ignace Ingianni. He published me in a few issues of *Simbolica*. By the way, the bills of lading that I would type up, using descriptions of the machine equipment, interested me and I thought that I would utilize that. I write about that in *Out of Ur*.[4]

AF: Yes, I read that.

RO: In that book, from *Not Be Essence That Cannot Be*, my first collection, it includes poems that were written in the late '50s.[5] There are poems I remember that did this.[6] Now Schlumberger, which is the name of some equipment...

AF: Their business is involved in drilling and oil production.

RO: And Schlumberger equipment was also described in these jobs I had. I had two jobs, and there was the language of bills of lading. The sewing machine company was called Macdowell Associates. And there was a very funny incident. Macdowell was the head of the firm. A very smart practical business man, who had a son-in-law working for him, and the son in law...I don't know if this is relevant.

AF: It's all relevant.

RO: Of course it's relevant. I was writing poetry! Oddly enough, when there was time at work, and there was time, I would write poetry. But I was typing on the letterheads. So one day Fenton, the son-in-law, said, [she drops to sotto voce] "Rochelle, if you are going to do your poetry, don't use the letterheads, you use the yellow paper." Which was nice! And he's right! George said that was very kind, he didn't mind that I was writing poetry on their time, but he asked me not to use the letterheads.[7] 'Cause I certainly was, I was pulling out the letterheads and writing poetry. But the language of these bills of lading I found enriching and interesting.

AF: Were there other influences?

RO: Early on, I was aware of Joyce's *Finnegans Wake*. A teacher had explained the unconventional structure of the phrasing in that work, which struck me. When I was very young, my father had taken me to the Museum of Modern Art, and I saw the painting *White on White*, the off-white canvas in the fancy frame, and that struck me as very exciting [by Kazimir Malevich, 1918]. And Weegee, the photographer. And *Grimm's Fairy Tales*, I liked their energy, the terrible horrific energy.
AF: I know—terrible, horrible things happen.
RO: They are horrible. I was 10 or even younger with the *Grimm's Fairy Tales*.
AF: You were exposed to art early, in an unfiltered way.
RO: My uncle was a photographer. Sol, my mother's favorite brother. He was the one who brought the Weegee [Arthur Fellig] photographs to our home in Brooklyn. That was a wonderful, startling, shocking series of images to see.
AF: It takes not having censorious parents to be able to have access to such images as a child.
RO: It was because my uncle introduced them. I was totally fascinated; over and over I'd look at those startling images. I doubt if my mother paid much attention because her dear brother had brought the book for the family. My father taking me to museums, my father respected culture; what I focused on was that very avant-garde image.
AF: You joined the Poetry Society of America at a young age, at 20.
RO: Before I became a member of the Poetry Society of America, I worked for the Poetry Society of America. I worked for a very strange, bitter, and highly confident atheist who was against all religion. His name was Gustav Davidson.[8] He was the head of the Poetry Society of America, which was in a crummy little office in Manhattan someplace, and he was a constant smoker. But he read my poetry and he thought there was something there, but then he gave me an anthology. He said, "Copy these forms!" Because I wasn't doing forms, I was already experimenting. And he probably thought there was some primitive native energy there that had to be controlled.
AF: Channeled, conventionalized.
RO: That's right. But what was interesting about Gustav Davidson, I'm trying to make the connection with these periods where I am using the machine language. The machine language started at my very first job, where I remember I was wearing a bouffant skirt with crinoline, which is like from the dinosaur age. However, something was going on with the language, that I enjoyed putting in different relationships. Making poems with the material of that language, which was not done. Marjorie [Perloff, poetry scholar] has called it, and maybe others, "proto language." As in The Language Poets.
AF: How did you feel about Gustav Davidson's telling you to adhere to formal poetic structures?

INTERVIEW WITH ROCHELLE OWENS *Friedman*

RO: I heard it, I took the book, but it didn't make an impact that I should do it. Because at that period I was aware of Dylan Thomas, and there was this energy and unusual language.

AF: I love Dylan Thomas's poetry. There is something wild, exciting; they feel like poems you discover, you don't just read them.

RO: That's right.

AF: And then there is all that mysterious Welshness going on because one doesn't really know what "Welsh" is. Because it's so obscure.

RO: Yes, the rhythms, and the sensibility, but on the other hand there was something that for me at least that transcended that. Like the phrase "the force that through the green fuse drives the flower." Well the rhythms are certainly lyrical and Welsh-y, British, but the sense is very primal and archaic.

AF: Yes. Who else figures in here as an influence on your early poetry?

RO: I also loved William Blake. And I had acquired the habit of writing. I do remember one time, this is probably 1956 or '57, I wrote what I considered a perfect stanza, and it was modelled on Byron. [Laughter from both Owens and Friedman.] So here's a perfect stanza and it's modelled on "She walks in beauty..." And I looked at it again and I felt an ennui. My eyelids became heavy. And I felt bored, and pissed, and annoyed, so then I realized No, no, I have to play around, without consciously saying, "I have to play around," but if I have this job constantly utilizing interesting language with machines... That was a beginning.

AF: What was your awareness of yourself at this point? Did you have a very clear idea that you were a poet, that you were creative, that you were going to write?

RO: That's a very good question. I had started writing, but not constantly, at around 14 and half. I remember the poem I wrote. I was smoking, I was smoking cigarettes at 14 and a half. I remember this though. I had crushed the cigarette. "As I sat and watched the dying ember, as a waning light." It was like that, it was short. But later on, how did I think of myself as a poet? Well, I studied ballet. For a long time I wanted to be a ballet dancer, but I did not have the stamina or the focus for the ballet. But I loved to watch the best dancer, and I loved to hear the French descriptions, the French words, and the long-playing records of Schubert. So now, in terms of when I thought of myself as a writer, I think I seriously began to think of myself as a writer at around probably 19. Because I had been married to this person, David. All of his friends were visual artists, and I loved the way they talked about art. At that time I *did* think of myself as a poet, but they didn't sound like poets. They expressed themselves more interestingly I thought. I intuited that in some way they talked about space because they were visual artists, not poets. And I liked the way they talked about creativity and art. Machines and bills of lading had made me aware of the possibility of juxtaposition and non-poetic language.

AF: I would call it radical juxtaposition.

RO: I like radical. I did not yet know other poets except for my reading, but later on I got to know lots of poets. We are talking about in the '50s. We are talking about when I was 17, 18, and because I met the poets, lots of poets, around 1960 [when Owens is 24], and more in 1962 and '63. Roi [LeRoi Jones] had published my poem in an issue of *Yugen* that I believe came out in 1960, so that means I knew him then, and Allen [Ginsberg] who referred me to him.[9]

AF: How did you first encounter Allen Ginsberg?

RO: It was a letter. I had been with him later on in the '70s, at poetry readings. We read together many places, and I'd also see him around. But in the late 1950s I sent him some poems, and he wrote to me and he said, "Send your poems." It is a wonderful letter, it starts, "Abracadabra!" That's how he starts it. Meaning the poems had this magic. "Dear Rochelle, Abracadabra! Send your poems to *Yugen*." Now when he came out to Oklahoma to read, much later, we were living there, and George was head of the university English department, and I was an adjunct, teaching creative writing. Allen came out and I introduced him, this was in the '80s. I introduced him before his reading. We also read together in New York and at a festival in Michigan in 1974. That was good. Ed Dorn was there. Does that name ring a bell?

AF: Yes, fine poet, somewhat Beat, associated with the Black Mountain poets.

RO: He would be considered one of the Beats?

AF: He counts. We'll take him.

RO: But I am glad you are not putting us all in that rigid frozen refrigerator.

AF: Of fixed category. "Beat." No. I have been very drawn to women writers from this period. I have written about Joanne Kyger, Diane di Prima...

RO: Di Prima is one year older than me.

AF: When you bring all of those interesting poets into the picture because their work is vivid and diverse, then we have something else to deal with, we have more complexity, we don't have a rigid category. There is nothing wrong with focusing on just Jack Kerouac, Allen Ginsberg, Gregory Corso, and that's fine, lots of people do that. But you bring these other writers in and you have a more interesting event going on and it gets more complicated around the edges, which I like.

RO: Absolutely!

AF: There's ongoing and new material, there are these book-length works [by di Prima, Anne Waldman; new work by Kyger and Owens] that should be studied by scholars and introduced to students. And only if a writer welcomes or merits a certain classification does it make sense to apply that, although you can explore their work in that context, to see what you can learn. To bring feminist critique to bear on writing can be helpful for me to make sense of it in a very specific way, but it doesn't mean that it's the only way to read that work; it just means that I found some fruitful connections doing that.

RO: Absolutely.

INTERVIEW WITH ROCHELLE OWENS   *Friedman*

AF: Let's move to the era of *Futz*, your play that became a film.[10] Researching this, I came across the era's Off-Off-Broadway venues, underground cinema, and art houses.

RO: I was working at Parke-Bernet auction galleries when I started that play. I started around 22 and I probably finished when I was 23, and the original text is written again at work. I was working at the auction galleries, on Madison Avenue in the [area of the] 70s, and this was in the year 1958. I worked there two a half years. People would go through and bid; Greta Garbo was there—I sound like an antique!—and Katharine Hepburn. Not at the same time. But it was a very prestigious place for people who were famous and affluent to acquire beautiful objects and art. Now what I do remember is that I was typing a first draft on the daily calendar of the auction place. Each day on the back on the blank page, each day between sales, I'd be typing.

AF: It was the auction house scrap paper for you.

RO: Yes that's right. In this case, it was the daily calendar. And then at home I would get very involved in it. As far as the language that I think of when I think back on *Futz*, I do realize it was quite courageous. In fact, some of my early work I think of as an organic discovery. In a mature work by a mature poet or playwright, if they have it to begin with and if they retain it, it's always a new authentic journey. Because a lot of poets have not changed their work in decades. So they find a form, and don't change. And I won't and can't do that.

AF: And that's definitely why "experimental," "avant-garde," those are apt terms, appropriate terms to apply to your work. What is the earliest play that you associate with your recognition of yourself as a playwright?

RO: *Futz* was my very first play that I ever wrote. But by the way, do you know that *Beclch* was a scandal in the city of Philadelphia?

AF: No. I knew about *Futz*. But I don't know that background about *Beclch*.

RO: It premiered here in Philadelphia.

AF: It's a very strong, very funny play.

RO: In 1966 it premiered. The director was Andre Gregory who is still alive. An enfant terrible! And the play was reviewed, which you should look up.[11] But *Beclch* caused a scandal in Philadelphia, it became the subject of church sermons, it was a lively and incredible production, and there was a dance company, I don't know if it still exists, Arthur Hall's Dance Company of Philadelphia, an African American dance company which provided wonderful spectacle of dance in this production that Andre Gregory did. It was done at the Theatre of the Living Arts, which later became another venue. In the middle-1960s it was a theatre.

AF: Now they have live music there. [AF mentions different Beat Generation writers to establish connections.]

RO: Absolutely. There is overlap. I knew [Michael] McClure very well. Our

paths crossed, he had written a play, a little after I had, a cowboy play. We read together also.
AF: Did you find any affinities with McClure and his use of sound?
RO: My thought is that he has never really changed his style.
AF: Ginsberg you mentioned.
RO: Allen was wonderful.
[Both agree that he was a provocateur.]
AF: And LeRoi Jones?
RO: LeRoi, what a complex person, I was just reflecting. Every now and then, LeRoi and I, when I lived on 606 West 16th Street, we would have these long conversations. He was a totally different person from Amiri Baraka. He was married to Hettie, whom I loved, and they had two little girls. The kind of communication LeRoi had with me on the telephone, talking about visiting Puerto Rico or Cuba, it was cozy, it was like two good friends. He was calm and kind, with none of his later politics.
AF: He published your poetry.
RO: And I published one of his plays. *Spontaneous Combustions*, it was a new play. I also included a new play from Adrienne Kennedy. I do like her work. And as you know her work is not naturalistic at all, so she too was influenced by the European avant-garde.
AF: How about Hettie Jones, because you knew her in the various phases of LeRoi Jones.
RO: In her book *How I Became Hettie Jones*, she mentions a time I was there for a party. Which she remembers distinctly, which we all do, when Fee Dawson and Joel Oppenheimer, they brutalized me with their misogynistic, nasty talk. I had a job, I had to dress respectfully, and I dropped in on Roi and Hettie. And *they* were there, doing the drunken, shitty, woman-putting-down number that was very popular.[12] And Hettie was witness to it, it looked like she was nursing one of the infants, or holding one of her little tots. Now she wrote about what happened differently from what I remember, in her book there is this wonderful scene where she remembers that day. And I too wrote about it. She said, "Rochelle's face turned bright red and she looked like she was going to cry." No. But she probably was right about how I looked, I remember getting very angry and pissed. I remember Fee Dawson and that gross, pseudo-Richard Burton, nasty, drunken, scornful, mocking women and their breasts, that greedy male obnoxious behavior. I remember him saying, because in my work clothes I looked quite bourgeois, "Why don't you draw out your wallet and draw a check so you can buy one of my paintings?" But Hettie remembered that "[h]e tried to look up Rochelle's dress. And her face turned bright red."
AF: You don't strike me as a crier. Maybe somebody who would have gotten angry.
RO: But mainly Hettie had a very sympathetic take on it. She had a kind of

empathetic passionate thing. She saw me as vulnerable, which I was! And she was. So she defended me. She said, "She's a wonderful poet, and Roi's putting her in *Yugen* too." She said that to Fee.
AF: That's a wonderful defense.
RO: Years later at Paul Blackburn's memorial, Fee was there and I brought up the incident. But he never remembered it….the insults. Now, Diane di Prima, I don't know how she dealt with it. But she was a certain kind of earth mother.
AF: Even then when you were both so young, she's already an earth mother?
RO: She had a lot of children! And I think she did have an earthiness—at that time that was one of the things which a creative woman could identify with. Diane did. It was generational, maybe it was even part of her Italian heritage.
AF: And Janine Pommy Vega?
RO: Janine Pommy Vega, as far as I knew, never wanted to be an earth mother.
AF: When did your path cross with hers?
RO: I knew her in New York. She was a very good friend of my friend Rochelle Rathner. I have a memory of Janine at a poetry reading at St. Mark's church in protest of the Vietnam War. She is a tawny-blonde in denim jeans. Is she part roller derby amazon and part jungle queen? She sure the hell looked it. She is sitting cross-legged on the floor reading and talking her poems in a working class New Jersey accent, frequently including a favorite phrase at the time, "yeah man." She was generous and idealistic—and I'm glad that I knew her.
AF: You mentioned that Anne Waldman is ten years younger.
RO: Yes, so if anything I influenced Waldman.
AF: You have comfortably sidestepped categorization. You are not uncomfortable that this interview is in the context of a Beat Studies journal.
RO: NO! Not at all! You have made it clear that the Beat category is amorphous. And I do share the time period, of being against literary tradition, against the stifling conformity, and against the three—Pack, Hall, and Simpson—who were very much trying to sanctify the homogenization of American poetry.[13]
AF: That's a great phrase.
RO: I wrote it down! And we who were urgently descendants of Blake, not that we wrote in that tradition, but the organic love of the nature of the evolution of poetry, which is to make it new, as Ezra Pound said.
AF: Also in some ways it comes down to, it is a little simplistic, but the idea of the Apollonian imposition of a strict tradition, versus a Dionysian spirit. I have always found the Dionysian much more exciting, the unexpected, celebratory, the potential for a bacchanal to break out at any time. And to me that verve is very much in a lot of your work, which is also about defying convention, and certainly standardized forms. Not being afraid to flout order. I find that exciting and brave. So who did you find who was perhaps a kindred spirit in theater?

Rochelle Owens, 2011. Photographer: George Economou.

RO: Maria Irene Fornés, who we called Irene. I knew her well. She was intuitive, rightly suspicious, and always wise. When The New York Theatre Strategy, a playwrights' cooperative, premiered my play *Kontraption* in 1975, Irene worked diligently both as costume designer and publicity director. She was a true visionary who enjoyed gender-bending her attire. She could also do a hilarious imitation of Fidel Castro jabbing his fingers into the heart of the U.S.A. I loved Irene Fornés's plays, and we were very good friends. *Kontraption*, which I think is interesting in terms of my concept at the time, which I still somehow believe holds true, shows relationships between women and men, co-dependencies, a critique of marriage, and the idealization of women and the absurd hideous debasement that women will experience because of this idealization.

INTERVIEW WITH ROCHELLE OWENS   *Friedman*

AF: Wrestling with this idea of the category of the Beat Generation, of a group of specific writers, I read some of them as riding a wave of success of being affiliated or included in this category. There seem to be some who chose not to distance themselves from that definition, instead of finding some way to throw that off and move in a new direction.

RO: What you are talking about is something that I disdain, writers who I consider careerists. What I am interested in is leaving an important body of work. And so one's time is spent in front of the computer. Rather than being on committees and award panels. Some poets are very successful, but they don't have that much work. So there is the difference. The people who are focused on maximizing career enrichment, and they are not interested in the art with that intensity of developing and experimenting and journeying.

AF: In studying Jack Kerouac's work, it is clear he became very uncomfortable with the attention and fame, and he just wanted to write.

RO: My very good friend Joy Walsh had a magazine *Moody Street Irregulars*; she was a devotee of Kerouac, a very gifted woman, very learned. I think she had some kind of romantic idealization of Kerouac and she loved the writing. She also was a huge supporter of my work. I met her in 1974, there was a reading I participated in, Ginsberg was there, Orlovsky was there. For me the Beat poets, as a definition, it was a time period where we were against a literary establishment. But it was inclusive. Hopefully it was inclusive. I don't think a category should be gelled or fixed. One should be like Sampson and break the chain.[AF directs the conversation to the material Rochelle Owens is currently working on.]

AF: How would you describe this current project?

RO: It's my long poem in progress, *Hermaphropoetics*. Rare but real. Accidents of art and nature in which the senses entwine. A series of poems inspired by spores, fruiting bodies, rupture, comfort with the rottenness. Metamorphosis, irregular sprouting of new neurological connections leads to the process of writing and living. Poetic meanings that lay in wait underground.

AF: I already read the part that is online.[14]

RO: Yes, six poems are online. A publisher is waiting to receive the manuscript. I did have 90 pages but I edited it down. I am very engrossed in it at the moment. Really interested and involved. [AF's interview request came just as that editor was pressing to see Rochelle's new work.] I said, when it is ready I will send it, but I am doing a very important interview! I will send it when it is ready, later on. And getting to say that was wonderful!

AF: That was clearly my karma for that day. I thank Rochelle Owens for being so incredibly generous with her time.

Notes

[1] A bill of lading is a document issued by a carrier which details contents of a shipment of merchandise, and conveys title of that shipment to a specified party. They are not considered to be innately poetic or even vaguely literary.

[2] From *Simbolica*, circa 1959:

> *Salt, Core, Nucleus and Heart*
> Can I in sin on august green
> Black-judge the beak I worship
> For anatomy and obscenity (nebulous)
> Powwow are skilled up like
> Salt, core, nucleus and heart.

[3] See Rochelle Owens, "Autobiography," *rochelleowens.org*.
[4] Rochelle Owens, *Out of Ur: New & Selected Poems 1961-2012*, Bristol, UK: Shearsman Books, 2013. Print.
[5] Rochelle Owens, *Not Be Essence That Cannot Be*, New York: Trobar, 1961. Print.
[6] *Not Be Essence* has several examples of Owens's machine-influenced experiments in language. The book's first page opens as follows:

> *Yields*
>   *(Which see)*
>   *Azzas*
> *See which*
> *Picker-tool*
> *Azzas*
> *Wielding*
> *A a growing*
> *Iso-*
> *Lation.*

[7] This is Rochelle's current husband, George Economou, poet, translator, and literary scholar.
[8] Gustav Davidson was executive secretary of the Poetry Society of America from 1949 to 1965.
[9] *Yugen* was the little magazine published by LeRoi and Hettie Jones, from their apartment in New York; the work of numerous Beat writers appeared in it.

INTERVIEW WITH ROCHELLE OWENS　　　*Friedman*

[10] *Futz* ran for 233 performances at the Actors Playhouse in New York. When it closed, *Beclch* was already running Off-Off-Broadway.

[11] I did. While *Futz* prompted a Canadian court case on obscenity charges (which is discussed in my forth-coming chapter on Owens's plays in Debra Geis, ed., *Beat Drama*, to be published by Methuen), *Beclch* drew a cacophony of protests from both the board of the Theatre of the Living Arts, which produced it, and from local and national press. When the play transferred to New York, it arrived with the city's first-ever official bar to anyone under the age of 14. Director Andre Gregory maintained later that the production did not lead to his firing from the TLA ("Taking a Trip With Andre and His 'Alice,'" interview with Elenore Lester, *The New York Times*, Nov 1, 1970). Within show business, Lester reported, it was widely thought that Gregory, "[t]he 'wild man,'" had offended an influential member of the Philadelphia theater's board with (of all things!) Saul Bellow's *The Last Analysis*, and later more members were unnerved by Gregory's uninhibited staging of Rochelle Owens's baroque jungle fantasy, *Beclch*." Interestingly, *Time* magazine featured a prominent review, which praised the "stunning" work of the Arthur Hall dancers and side-stepped the scandal completely.

[12] Owens refers to Beat-era writer and artist Fielding "Fee" Dawson (1930-2002). The episode is recounted in Hettie Jones's *How I Became Hettie Jones*, New York: Grove Press, 1996, 111. Print.

[13] Owens here denotes a trio of critics whose anthologizing and rejections of specific types of poetry in this era were assessed in some quarters as widely stultifying; see *The New Poets of England and America*, edited by Donald Hall, Robert Pack, and Louis Simpson. New York: Meridian Books, 1957. This was followed by *New Poets of England and America: Second Selection*, which Hall and Pack edited in 1962, also published by Meridian.

[14] Excerpts from Owens's work-in-progress, *Hermaphropoetics*, can be found at <rochelleowens.org>.

Reviews

Crowded by Beauty: The Life and Zen of Poet Philip Whalen
David Schneider
(Oakland: University of California Press, 2015)

This is an important book: an important book for San Francisco Renaissance and Beat Studies; an important book for American Buddhist studies; and an important book for students of American literature and culture in general, for, as happens with good biography, it moves beyond the life of the individual under question and captures, to quote from the title of one of Philip Whalen's poems, the "Paideuma" of post-World War II America, and, to a lesser extent, occupied Japan as experienced through the lives of sympathetic Americans.[1] According to Hugh Kenner, paideuma equates to "a people's whole congeries of patterned energies, from their 'ideas' down to the things they know in their bones, not a *Zeitgeist* before which minds are passive."[2] *Crowded by Beauty: The Life and Zen of Poet Philip Whalen* attempts to "place Philip Whalen, among his friends, in American letters of the second half of the twentieth century" and points "to his role in helping establish Zen Buddhism in the West" (146). *Crowded by Beauty* is a long-anticipated and much overdue book about one of the most influential yet under-read poets of the last sixty years.

David Schneider, the author of this, the first full-length biography on Whalen, is not new to the genre; in 2007 he published *Street Zen: The Life and Work of Issan Dorsey*. A friend and colleague of Whalen's, Issan Dorsey was the founding abbot of the Hartford Street Zen Center in San Francisco, where Whalen lived, taught, and practiced from 1988 to 1996. *Crowded by Beauty* was initially begun in the early 1980s as a journal Schneider wrote while practicing with Whalen at the Zen Center over a period of twelve years. According to the author, twenty years after writing his journal—and shortly before Whalen's death in 2002—he typed up the manuscript and then, after waiting "a respectful time after his death," began shopping it around to publishers (xi). Not surprisingly in today's academic publishing market, Schneider was initially unable to locate an interested publisher because neither he nor Whalen were "famous enough" to apparently merit the investment (xi). Luckily, UC Press shortly thereafter contacted Schneider for just such a book. With an adept hand at scholarship and captivating storytelling, Schneider's narrative draws heavily upon Whalen's correspondence and journals, which are primarily held at Berkeley's Bancroft Library, Columbia's Rare Book and Manuscript Library, and the Philip Whalen Papers in Reed College's Oral History Project Collection and Special Collections in the Eric V. Hauser Memorial Library. *Crowded by Beauty* also mines the online Naropa Poetics Audio Archive, as well as Schneider's personal interviews with Joanne Kyger, Richard Baker, Michael McClure, Gary Snyder, and many others, including Michael Rothenberg, editor of *The Collected Poems of Philip Whalen*, and Norman Fisher, Whalen's literary executor.

Unlike most biographies, the narrative of *Crowded by Beauty* does not proceed chronologically until midway through the book. Rather, after opening with a brief chronology and introductory chapter, Schneider presents Whalen in Chapters 2 through 6 as seen in relation to specific friends: Chapter 2, Whalen and Ginsberg; Chapter 3, Whalen and Kerouac; Chapter 4, Whalen and Snyder; Chapter 5, Whalen and Kyger; Chapter 6, Whalen and McClure. The narrative then becomes chronological in Chapters 7 through 15. This is, as Schneider explains in his introduction, an unusual way to write a biography. As a practicing Buddhist himself, Schneider calls on his readers to embrace "a certain looseness or spaciousness, a flexibility of mind," because inherent in writing the biography of a "highly trained Buddhist monk . . . lurks the Buddhist conviction . . . that none of this can be pinned down; that it is all . . . empty" (7). A second theoretical framework informing *Crowded by Beauty* is that of Tibetan spiritual biographies, which present the "the same story told on three levels: outer, inner, and secret" (7). Likewise, "another three-part division" from the Buddhist tradition also informs the text's structure—that of getting at a person through sectioning them into body, speech, and mind. As Schneider says, "[t]his scheme allows a picture to be made at any point in a person's life, without slipping into the fallacy of saying, 'This is who they actually *are*.' Who they are emerges, almost magically, from the collection of bits" (8). As he later says of the first half of the book, it is "clear that Philip's personal connections *were* the story," and, like Whalen's poetry itself, *Crowded by Beauty* is "an asynchronous mixture of affection and events" (188). One could perhaps also say this about Barry Gifford and Lawrence Lee's *Jack's Book: An Oral Biography of Jack Kerouac*.

Crowded by Beauty is not a literary biography; Schneider does "not attempt much literary criticism, apart from praise. Philip's poetry appears, but in support of, or in explanation of, his life, not the other way around" (xiv). Whalen's often seemingly indecipherable verse does indeed help support and explain his life as Schneider employs it throughout the book. The first five chapters of the biography proper, all of which are relatively short—the longest, on Snyder, is only forty-four pages long. Chapter 2, "Banjo Eyes," opens with the serendipitous meeting of Whalen, Kerouac, and Ginsberg just a few days before the 6 Gallery reading. In just over twenty pages, the chapter chronicles Whalen and Ginsberg's friendship from inception through Whalen's having to cope with Ginsberg's death in 1997. Between these events, Schneider discusses the 6 Gallery reading, with a focus on Whalen; Whalen and Ginsberg's developing commitments to Buddhism; Ginsberg's tireless help in promoting Whalen's poetry to publishers back east; and their time teaching together at Naropa. Of the latter, Schneider lays out some interesting differences in the two friends' teaching styles: Ginsberg was "voluble, dominating, confessional, energetic, demanding," whereas "Whalen preferred to open things out from a poem and then wander a bit" (28). Further, "Allen seemed to feel that students could be led. Philip felt students must be pushed to find out things for themselves" (29).

Considering that Whalen's relationships with Jack Kerouac and Gary Snyder have been chronicled in several book-length biographies, I will jump forward to Chapter 5, "Your Heart Is Fine," which focuses on the sometimes tumultuous relationship between Whalen and Joanne Kyger. Here too, Schneider's use of Whalen and Co.'s rich unpublished correspondence pays off to create an interesting and informative picture of two important mid-century American poets. Both Whalen and Kyger shared an affinity for Snyder, Zen, going to Japan, and, in the case of Whalen, a romantic affinity for the other. Though the two never consummated their relationship, according the Schneider, it was not due to Whalen's lack of trying (nor Snyder's lack of encouragement). In Chapter 5 we learn more about Whalen's *undetermined* (for the lack of a better word) sexuality. "No one among Philip's oldest friends," according the Schneider, "can ever remember Philip's having a girlfriend or boyfriend . . . If there is ever any name that people suggest, even skeptically or half-disbelievingly . . . it is Joanne's name, and that because of the connections Philip made and deepened with her in 1959" (101). Kyger confirms this, saying, "I never heard of *anybody* who *ever* said they had a physical relationship with him" (105).

One of the most intriguing aspects of their relationship presented by Schneider was their mutual interest in the Buddhist notion of emptiness. "The explicit knowledge of nonexistence makes a strange bond," he says, "but it's one they had" (122). In a discussion of several of their poems dealing with this topic, Schneider explains:

> Joanne came to share with Philip an experience of mind comparable to a broad field, more loosely organized (and more highly populated) than suits a standard "ego." Yet she also realized—more clearly than Philip—that a person had to function practically to live in the world. . . . As with Philip's work, Joanne's playfulness and her hard-won light touch may disguise from some readers her profundity. She did not spend thirty years as a Zen monk, but like Philip, she pursued truth—dharma—with remarkable persistence. (123-124)

Chapter 5 presents one of the more philosophically interesting discussions in the book, and it is here that the reader really benefits from Schneider's own profound and subtle understanding of—and ability to explain—the ephemeral nature of emptiness and Mind. Schneider poignantly notes that the last poems Whalen had read aloud to him by Rick London on his deathbed were from Kyger's then recently-published *Again: Poems 1989-2000*.

It is in Chapter 7, the midpoint of the biography, where we begin to see "[m]ore standard bibliographic chapters—childhood, army service, college education, sojourns in Japan, ordination as a Buddhist priest, work with his spiritual teacher, his own teaching, and his death—now appear in order" (146). Indeed, for most of the remainder of the book the reader is presented with a more traditional biography, one that covers a diverse cultural and spiritual landscape. In Chapters 7 through 9, which cover Whalen's life from 1923-1951, we meet several people who played instrumental roles in Whalen's developing poetics as a young man—from Stanworth Beckler to Lew Welch and William Carlos Williams among others. Beckler, a fellow private in basic training with Whalen in Biloxi, Mississippi, taught Whalen the basics of counterpoint and harmony. Decades later, during a Naropa lecture in 1976, Whalen said, "My sense of the shape of words, and how they go together, and how blocks of words will go together to make a stanza or make a chunk of poetry, is drawn almost entirely from music" (164). Another major influence on Whalen's (and Snyder's) thinking and writing was Lloyd Reynolds, the well-known professor of calligraphy and graphic arts at Reed College who both Snyder and Whalen have spoken at length about over the years. In Whalen's work we see, through Reynolds's "cultural patrilineage," their "[l]ove of nature, sharp critique of industrial materialism, admiration for eighteenth-century literature, an exhortation to make and do" (173). Like so many artists and academics during the McCarthy reign, Reynolds was suspended from Reed for refusing to answer the questions posed by the House on Un-American Activities Committee. Another Reedite accused of communism, though he was no longer living on the West Coast, was Lew Welch, who Schneider discusses at the end of his chapter on Reed.

Chapters 10 and 11 briefly return to "an asynchronous mixture of affection and event" to move the narrative forward into Whalen's next major friendship and stage of his life—that with Richard Baker and the Zen Center. These chapters, which focus on the years 1959-1971, cover "a swell of poets, painters, peaks, parks, printers and publishers" in a mere thirty-five pages (188). Schneider's unusual approach works, though, because in not setting out to move chronologically from birth to death *a la* traditional biography, he is able to reconstruct Whalen's life in and out of time, for "time can run in both directions; that, strictly speaking, everything is happening at once" (147). The first of these chapters explores Whalen's relationships with Donald Allen and LeRoi Jones; the early 1960s, which led to his second East

Coast reading tour, continued poverty, and the writing of a good deal of poetry; the Longshoreman's Hall reading with Snyder and Welch, and the Vancouver Poetry Conference, among other things.

Chapter 11, which addresses some of the same dates (1965-1971) as the previous chapter, follows Whalen back and forth from, as the title tells us, "Japan, Bolinas, Japan, Bolinas." Whalen's second stay in Kyoto, according to Schneider, is where "Philip begins to shift from what Gary Snyder called the 'seductive cultural fascination of old Japan' to actually 'hearing the message of the big Buddhist temples'" (219). Here Schneider points to two key experiences that moved him further towards formal practice: 1) "the manifest power of emptiness" he experienced trying to recite the Heart Sutra from memory while walking outside one day, and 2) contemplating his own impermanence while circumambulating Hyakuman Jinja and looking at a graveyard on a different occasion. Schneider quotes an interview with David Chadwick from *Cuke* online: "'I saw how things looked and started to cry... I told myself that what I've got to do is find a teacher and be a monk'" (220). Though he visited several different *rōshis* and halfheartedly continued to sit while in Kyoto, it was not until his return to Bolinas in the summer of 1971, at which time he was invited by the Bakers to move into the Zen Center shortly after Suzuki Roshi's death, that he finally took the steps to become a monk.

The remainder of the book (chapters 12 through 15) will be of particular interest to readers of earlier volumes on American Buddhism such as Michael Downing's *Shoes Outside the Door: Desire, Devotion, and Excess at San Francisco Zen Center* (2001), Helen Tworkov's *Zen in America: Five Teachers and the Search for an American Buddhism* (1994), and Rick Fields's *How the Swans Came to the Lake: A Narrative History of Buddhism in America* (1992). Recognizing the work done by Downing in *Shoes Outside the Door*, Schneider does not set out here to rewrite the scandal of 1983-84 that tore the Zen Center asunder; rather, he addresses the scandal and its aftermath in passing as it pertains directly to Whalen, including his time in Santa Fe and back in California at the Hartford Street Zen Center.[3]

Baker and Whalen met in mid-1950s in New York through their mutual acquaintances Donald Allen and John and Margot Doss. Even before meeting, Baker admired Whalen's poetry because his "experience... was not convergent with the usual way the world [is] described or viewed" (229). Baker further elaborated to Schneider in an interview: "There was a greater realization in his practice. Some of his poems show the kind of insight and knowledge of the world I call realization. He was able to find it in literature, but he wasn't able to find it in his life, until quite late in his practice" (265). According to Schneider, one of the things that might have waylaid Whalen's realization was his at times frustrating relationship with Baker, who kept putting off making his friend's dharma transmission official by not filling out the requisite paperwork for a year after his ordination in July 1987.[4]

No longer in this state of limbo, Whalen returned to his beloved West Coast the following year and moved into the Hartford Street Zen Center, where he resided and served first as head of training and then as abbot until he retired due to his poor health in 1996. The remaining five years of Whalen's life, as presented in the final five pages of the book, show a close-knit and compassionate community of friends taking turns at Whalen's bedside and working to raise funds to cover expenses. He passed away on June 26, 2002, at Laguna Honda Hospice.

If there is a downside to *Crowded by Beauty*, it is indeed the fact that it is not a literary biography. This reader was very much looking forward to the possibility of having a critical volume to set on the shelf alongside Michael Rothenberg's monumental *The Collected Poems of Philip Whalen*—not a compendium, mind you, but a book with more close readings, which, when we are talking about Whalen, also necessitates a good deal of philosophical discussion. Though it never purports to provide this kind of in-depth exploration, *Crowded by Beauty* has certainly laid the groundwork for such a volume to come, for Schneider presents us—"almost magically, from the collection of bits" from letters, journals, conversations, interviews, and personal experiences with Whalen—the ideas and "patterned energies" of this singular poet's life and times. Schneider's is a detailed, considered, and far-reaching portrait. As Joanne Kyger says in a blurb on the dust jacket, Schneider "transmits the delight and wisdom of this poet's bountiful spirit." For that, this Whalen devotee is most grateful.

—Todd Giles, *Midwestern State University*

Notes

[1] "The Slop Barrel: Slices of the Paideuma for All Sentient Beings," *The Collected Poems of Philip Whalen*. Middletown, CT: Wesleyan UP, 2007, 56-62. Print.
[2] Hugh Kenner, *The Pound Era*. U of California P, 1973, 507. Print.
[3] The Zen Center scandal centered on Baker's extramarital relationships with female students. Baker resigned as abbot and in 1984 moved with Whalen and a handful of other devotees in tow to found a new Zen center in Santa Fe.
[4] Dharma transmission, according to Baker's introduction to Whalen's *Canoeing Up Cabarga Creek*, "means to receive and realize Mind, spirit, and essential teachings of your teacher and lineage" (qtd. in Schneider 260).

REVIEWS   *Damon*

Elise Cowen: Poems and Fragments
Elise Cowen, edited by Tony Trigilio
(Boise: Ahsahta Press, 2014)

Derek Jarman on finishing reading a biography of Allen Ginsberg: "I do love *Howl*, but I couldn't help thinking [the Beat phenomenon, the bio] was all a palaver, America scrutinizing its navel, and the myth-making Beats? Quite an ordinary little bunch seriously cultivating slender legends."

—*Modern Nature*

There were women, they were there, I knew them, their families put them in institutions, they were given electric shock. In the '50s if you were male you could be a rebel, but if you were female your families had you locked up. There were cases, I knew them, someday someone will write about them.

—*Gregory Corso,
from Stephen Scobie's account of the Naropa Institute tribute to Ginsberg,
July 1994*

Why do the Beats continue to fascinate, and does the special denominator "Beat Studies" do what we want it to do? What, for that matter, is the relationship of beat literature (lower case) and Beat Studies? Given these questions and the incontrovertible evidence that the Beats are what we would call, in contemporary terms, a "brand," around which "buzz" was created due to the efficiency of then-new media, as well as the indefatigable efforts of Allen Ginsberg to publicize his friends as a "boy gang" of raw but paradoxically well-read geniuses (Ginsberg cited by Johnson, xx), how is Beat writing to be valued or made meaningful in the context of the literary? Is this even a worthy endeavor? It seems to put those who identify as Beat scholars on the defensive, claiming on the one hand that the writing is good/ great literature as conventionally understood, and on the other hand that beats were up to something new, a *soi-disant* "uniquely American" take on the European *maudit* tradition (*avec* some U.S. transcendentalism thrown in), with a dose of African, via African American jazz, underworld culture, and what has come to be called "oraliture" (Petrilli and Ponzio 2001). Further, how are the lesser-known names and Beat members from aggrieved populations—people of color, minoritized genders and sexualities—to be treated within this still-wobbly, still-being-born movement from scholarly periphery to centrality and legitimacy? If Beat culture was, as is generally acknowledged, one of white men who embraced the underworld, how are the actual denizens of the underworld (by which I mean the world of under-privilege as well as the conventionally understood criminal edges of the demi-monde) to be treated?

As some readers of this journal know, I have a highly ambivalent relationship to the Beat Studies project, much like Derek Jarman whom I cite above. Some of the literature is thrilling, some of the hype is unbearable; some of the literature is trying too hard; some of the pathos of life-stories transcends the hype *and* the half-realized literary project. The half-realized is part of its appeal to my perhaps idiosyncratic aesthetic sensibilities. What has opened up for me the possibility of talking about the Beat movement in a way that does not aim to canonize its major writers, and that turns meaningful attention to the raw, the fragmentary, the broken, the unfinished, the underside of this underside of the canon is the legacy of cultural studies. This frankly partisan approach eschews literary evaluation altogether in favor of exploring and analyzing the "structures of feeling" (in Raymond Williams's influential phrase) and cultural artifacts (letters and other texts, fashion styles, domestic arrangements, and other para- and/or extra-textual phenomena) of historical moments and their subcultures of resistance, in order to draw attention to and valorize that resistance. While this might appear to diminish what is, in conventional litcrit and lithist terms, the "literary achievement" of the participants, the point is not so much to achieve, or to be recognized as having achieved, as to have the ambition to do so. (Iggy Pop's definition of a punk, for example, as someone whose glorious, heartfelt ambitions transcends his/her abilities, seems to resonate strongly with the double meaning embedded in the word "beat": blessed and defeated, as the example of Neal Cassady demanding that his collegiate friends teach him to understand Nietzsche suggests.) Let us be free from that debt to achievement as conventionally understood. Likewise, a critical approach that prioritizes neither the finished work nor authorial intention fully justifies publishing work that may not have been intended for publication. For aesthetic as well as ethical reasons, one can once again invoke Walter Benjamin's mandate that "nothing that has happened should be lost to history." One might ask, rather, why so much of the work is unfinished. Could it be that, because Elise Cowen was a woman, there was no network of publishers or influential mentors who took her seriously enough to help her? Or, for the same reason, her material resources did not offer her enough respite from daily chores or work for money for her to be able to write as conscientiously as she might have wanted? Or simply that, for the same reason, she lacked the confidence and self-esteem that publication or a higher artistic profile were ambitions that she was entitled to and/or could achieve? Or that, as a person with desires and yearnings illegible to the majority culture, she had few internal or external resources for even articulating a clear-cut path to literary recognition? These are among the puzzlements and challenges of confronting the work of a partially realized literary life, a partiality that mirrors the half-realized nature of the work itself as presented here.

With this in mind, we can read Elise Cowen's *Poems and Fragments* as a bit of legend made real, spirit and myth given tangible, palpable language that helps us grapple with the history of women poets in the U.S. twentieth century, women in the Beat scene, the treatment of mental instability—especially depression and drug psychosis—at mid-century, and Elise Cowen in particular. Ever since initial interest in the women Beats emerged through anthologies of critical essays and imaginative work in the mid-1990s, Cowen has been an appealing and enigmatic figure, legendary as one of Allen Ginsberg's few women lovers and typewriter transcriber of Ginsberg's masterpiece "Kaddish," warm and faithful friend to many women on the scene, gifted thinker and writer (years after Cowen's death, writer Janine Pommy Vega, herself a high school valedictorian, called Cowen the "smartest person [she] knew"), a rare and fine soul lost to some sort of psychosis or depression (possibly induced by alcohol, opiate and/or amphetamine overuse, though it is impossible to say with any certainty) and suicide (dramatically jumping through a seventh-storey, *locked* window) at 28.

The collection has been sensitively and thoroughly edited by Tony Trigilio, whose exhaustive research turned up a handwritten copy of the poems, circumventing Cowen's notoriously protective friend Leo Skir, who, believing himself to be Cowen's literary executor, alternately co-operated with and obstructed younger scholars wishing access to the dead poet's manuscript, of which Skir's was presumed to be the only copy. Of course, no such discovery is made solo, and Trigilio's accomplishment is no doubt the end result of many attempts by scholars involved in feminist reclamation projects, Beat aficionados, and other interested parties. Beat materials occupy a peculiar space along the continuum of popular/mass culture, powerful fandom (Johnny Depp) or familial interests (the Sampas family), hagiography and serious scholarship, and as many people who could be useful to these folks are dying or still living but either deliberately laying low (William Burroughs's step-daughter, for example) or are just now being seriously researched (Cowen or LuAnne Henderson, one of Cassady's wives), when hard artifacts surface it is usually the result of much networking and cooperation among interested parties, delicate negotiations, and good timing. Trigilio has presented his amazing discovery—the handwritten manuscript—the poems and fragments (which include snatches of unsent letters which appear on the same page as drafts), not in chronological order but in groupings according to theme, ending, of course, with death, a prominent figure in Cowen's work, as it is for many chronic depressives.

Cowen writes in the tradition of Emily Dickinson, Joanne Kyger, and Larry Eigner in her gravitation toward short, cryptic, intensely felt verses made up of arresting images, sensory perceptions, and often acute longing, the latter quality reminiscent of John Wieners. All evidence of a powerful, even ecstatic, interiority is here, albeit one that cannot seem to express itself with full abandon. There is a thwartedness to the language, which is both its power and its pathos. It seems to pull back at the last minute, perhaps in the interest of creating an interesting verbal artifact, from saying what needs to be said.

> You
> Stand in my heart
> as headlight
> The brown livingroom wall disappears
> And I
> Am a brown haired schoolgirl
> *The* is a regal word... (62)

And yet that half-formed verbal shard twinned with obliquely named torment—dare one call it love? Loneliness?—is what pulls me in. As with so much raw, unfinished work, the appeal lies in its appearance of being caught mid-process. It is quivering with life because the poet has not let it go yet, possibly cannot reconcile herself to the notion of anything being finished, because such a state approximates death, which is longed-for but at the same time dreaded, in case its arrival pre-empts the possibility that this overwhelming love-loneliness may be alleviated through a healing experience of requited emotion, which never arrives and might likely not be recognized if it did.

Much of the poetry addresses the liminal spaces between life and death, spaces in which dead materials can be brought back to life or otherwise made meaningful for everyday living.

> I took the skin of corpses
> And dyed them blue for dreams
> Oh, I can wear them everywhere
> I sat home in my jeans.
>
> I cut the hair of corpses
> And wove myself a sheath
> Finer than wool or silk I thought
> And shivered underneath... (33)

Despite its macabre aura, this poem spells out precisely what clothing is: made from skins, wool (sheep living and dead), silk (silkworms killed in the cocoon), and other matter. On the one hand, Cowen, in an era in which new synthetics are being hailed as miraculous alternatives to organic fabrics, reminds us of the gendered labor and routine "upcycling" involved in caring for the human at the most basic level. On the other hand, this is not a happy poem about domesticity as one might find in Gertrude Stein's descriptions of "Objects," "Food," and "Rooms," in which an unorthodox but stable and loving household is celebrated through close attention to the material adornments of that arrangement; or in Elizabeth Bishop's celebration of the "homely" and awkward female "Moose" as muse, in which animal spirits subtly aid humans to survive emotionally their confrontations with loss, parting, and displacement. The haunted ghoulishness of "I Took the Skin of Corpses" rather inhabits the world of Mary Shelley's *Frankenstein*, as Trigilio points out, and also Cowen's contemporary Helen Adam's murder ballads, specifically "I Love My Love," in which a uxoricide is in turn murdered by the animate strands of his dead wife's lush tresses ("the living fleece of her long bright hair"), which slips out of her grave and under his door, devouring him to the bone. The uncanny, uncomfortable underside of everyday practices in seedy bohemia comprise Cowen's domain, but in a far more intimate and personal way than similar material is handled in Ginsberg's or even Bob Kaufman's work. The emotions are rawer, the pain more directly addressed (again, Wieners is the closest analogue in the male panoply). In each of the earlier stanzas, attempts at survival and self-reliance (the latter a famously American virtue explicated in great detail by Emerson, one of the spiritual forerunners, in some senses, of the Beats), traditionally gendered-female skills (sewing, refashioning and mending) turns out to have been deployed in the interest of a futile and self-deluded vision that is as mundane as it is hopeless: going outdoors, finding companionship, keeping warm, enjoying the sun. As the poem progresses, the resiliency and cleverness of having been able to repurpose through grave-robbing turns into a vision of imprisonment by these very attempts at self-rescue: "Now when I meet the spirits / In whose trappings I am jailed / They buy me wine or read a book / No one can go my bail." While it is tempting to read this poem as an allegory for the futility of the newfound materialism of the 1950s and '60s, which was founded on imperialistically-expanded markets and the corpses, real and metaphorical, of subordinated Others, the abjection of the narrator suggests rather a sense that none of her bodily being ever really belonged to her; that she is living a life assembled from burdensome, carnal detritus (herself and not-herself) that enslaves her to the grave. While this type of dissociation (my body is / is not me) is not unusual in Beat writing, it takes on a particular valence when gender is brought to bear on the analysis.

And given the gendered realities of the 1950s and early '60s, when first-generation immigrants were under tremendous pressure to assimilate to their parents' desires for their upward social and economic mobility, Gregory Corso's intervention in the 1994 Naropa Conference cited above as counterpoint to Derek

Jarman's rueful ambivalence about the Beat legacy, comes, sadly, as no surprise: as a rule, in a ubiquitously hostile situation, the disenfranchised fare worse. Of course, Wieners, Ginsberg as well as his mother Naomi, Bob Kaufman, Carl Solomon, and many others were locked up, given shock treatments, or lobotomized; but in the intervening decades, a heroism has coalesced around the myth of Ginsberg's tale of encounter with Solomon in the psychiatric hospital that has fueled rather than stifled legend. Cowen's story has heretofore garnered no such heroic aura.

Among the many ways in which Cowen's work inhabits liminal space, this impulse toward the inside/outside, assimilation/refusal, upward/downwardness, and so forth, is the ghostliness, the hovering between the living and the dead. Trigilio devotes the entire final section to death-oriented poems, and given the poet's suicide, this is appropriate. But I also read this in-between-ness as a form of deterritorialization, a state of being semi-embodied. "I Took the Skin of Corpses" is only one of many poems that position the poet in a haunted continuum of life/death. "Your Fate Awaits Outside the Door" parlays an innocent, random fortune cookie fortune into an eerie auditory encounter with the other side; after answering two sets of knockings at her apartment door, the poet tugs at the door fumblingly to find "no one–but empty blue light weird on the tile floor." Through its skillful placement as the last poem in the volume, Trigilio connects the poem with a beckoning to/from death, a summons from the other side; however, it also functions as one of many poems that dwell in and on the interzones between embodiment, dissociation, and disembodiment. Middle class women during the 1950s and early '60s were alienated from their bodies through multiple mechanisms and discourses, including the medicalization of childbirth combined with the ongoing prohibition on legal and safe abortion, the prohibitions on breastfeeding and the commercialization of infant-nursing products, prohibitions on working "outside the home," i.e., earning an income that might enable them to control their material circumstances independently, and so forth. Women are not the only demographic who experienced this alienation: among others, African American Bob Kaufman writes about the split between consciousness/body movingly in "Would you wear my eyes?" and the queer, working-class John Wieners suggests it throughout *The Hotel Wentley Poems*; Earl Jackson has suggested that Burroughs's cut-up technique could be rooted in the dissociation of traumatic-because-strictly forbidden early same-sex encounters. Cowen's work shares with other Beats mentioned above (Wieners, Kaufman) the sense of deterritorialized, decentering self-othering that accompanies a traumatic relationship to the mainstream. But in Cowen's work, the interplay between the living and the dead, the extent to which birth and death are types of each other (for women both experiencing childbirth and being born themselves into a world of severely cramped possibilities, and in an era in which, while the reality of death in childbirth had much diminished, women routinely underwent total anesthesia—a simulation of death—for the birth process), the surrealism of floating between these worlds and sometimes inhabiting them simultaneously is palpable and powerfully affecting. Exploration of the body, and sexual relationships with (unattainable) men, becomes a way for an overprotected, bookish, Jewish girl to experience herself as redeemed ("Teacher—Your Body My Kabbalah" is a marvelous instantiation of Cowen's attempt to heal the rifts between language, gender, sexuality, the body, and the sacred), and then inevitably betrayed. Another powerful poem, "I wanted a cunt of golden pleasure," also strongly places Cowen among the ecstatics, yearning for a complete synthesis between mind, heart, soul and body in the act of love that is a "golden pleasure / purer than heroin... or heaven." The cunt, a very old word in English and still one of the most shocking when seen in print, becomes a holy grail, a vessel of alchemical transubstantiation from the mundane to the sacred through secular consummation of a love/sex relationship. The poet's body/heart/imagination becomes a series of spaces: a cunt, a couch, a double bed, a meadow, tidepool, a city...expanding to accommodate the lover, in whose arms in turn she rests "all night long." The plaintive "I wanted" and "Oh that I was" suggest that only in the poem does this come to be. Like her muse Allen Ginsberg, Cowen's response to postwar social death and alienation was to seek the velocity of a heavenward flight of desire that necessarily took its path through the muck and squalor of the illicit.

In this unfulfillable desire for disalienation, the broken rawness of the work, combined with the clear intelligence of the writer, forms a poignant and meaningful portrait of women's predicament in a bohemia that both welcomed and exploited them, that ambivalently recognized and suppressed their literary talents and ambitions.

—Maria Damon, *Pratt Institute*

Works Cited

Petrilli, Susan and Augusto Ponzio. "Telling Stories in the Era of Global Communication: Black Writing: Oraliture." *Research in African Literatures* 32:1 (Spring, 2001): 98-109. Print.

Conversations with Ken Kesey
Edited by Scott F. Parker
(Jackson: University Press of Mississippi, 2014)

The University Press of Mississippi's *Conversations* series, which compiles previously published interviews with world-renowned writers, has, over the years, provided not only new insights for scholars, but also entertaining reading for the general public. Keeping with this tradition, *Conversations with Ken Kesey*, edited by Scott F. Parker, collects seventeen interviews that range over forty years from 1959 to 1999, roughly spanning the period from the writing of *One Flew Over the Cuckoo's Nest* to shortly before Kesey's death on November 10, 2001. The earlier interviews appeared in underground press publications while the later in major literary and academic journals. Tracing this publication history allows readers to see Kesey's growing importance, canonization, and lionization as an American cultural figure, as well as an American writer. The collection's chronological organization also reveals Kesey's changing perceptions and pronouncements and, taken in total, portray a man of complex contradictions. Although Kesey's public persona never seemed to wear thin like that of his friend Hunter S. Thompson, the interviews work to make the split between Kesey the man and Kesey the performer somewhat clearer while persistently underscoring his position as a major touchstone for post-World War II American countercultures.

Throughout the interviews, Kesey cannily grounds his actions and fiction within the context of masculine performance and the great American myth of the expansive drive of the West. He applies his homespun American wisdom to the craft of writing as well as applying that clear-eyed approach to the often confusing, shifting world of writing and publishing. Repeatedly, Kesey relays to interviewers words that he attributes to his father—"good writing ain't necessarily good reading"—and to William Faulkner—"Ever so often the dog has to go against the bear just to keep calling itself the dog." Accurate attribution aside, much of Kesey's public image is clear within those phrases, but readers are left to determine if these texts are ever able to puncture the façade and reveal Kesey the person as well as Kesey the persona.

Parker's assemblage of interviews with Kesey depicts a man who resists being pigeonholed. In the early interviews, Kesey reveals Neal Cassady's influence on him through the idea of a life lived as an artistic endeavor. And the 1993 interview with *The Paris Review*, more than any of the others, works to place Kesey within the Beat pantheon, with Cassady as his great teacher and Ginsberg as his connection to Vik Lovell, who engineered Kesey's participation in the original LSD experiments conducted by the CIA at the Menlo Park Veterans Hospital in California. By the time of this interview, a 58-year-old Kesey is reflective, especially when it comes to Cassady, who had then been dead for a quarter of a century. The most important lesson learned from Cassady, Kesey relates, is also "the most ironic: most of what is important cannot be taught except by experience. His [Cassady's] most powerful lesson behind the rap was not to dwell on mistakes" (151).

But Kesey himself was never entirely comfortable with the Beat label. His famous comment that he was too young to be a Beatnik and too old to be a hippie—repeated here in the *Salon* magazine interview (173)—is sometimes understood to be rueful, but after reading the collected interviews, one may conclude that it was a warning to readers and scholars not to attempt to categorize him quite so easily. The man we see depicted here often has little patience for interviewers who think that they know and understand him or who seem to believe that since he *is* Ken Kesey, he must unthinkingly accept all ideas that bubble up from the underground.

Pulitzer-Prize winning cartoonist Tony Auth, who began his work in the underground American publications of the '60s, told NPR's *Fresh Air* program in 1988 that it was easier working for mainstream than counterculture newspapers because the "underground editors tended to think they knew the truth." Many of the earlier Kesey interviews are also drawn from the small underground press of the time and, as one might suspect, they carry its bias. Take, as an example, the 1970 interview with the *Ann Arbor Argus*, which finds Kesey in a combative mood, starting his side of the conversation with "I hate interviews" (43), and challenging the interviewer's questions on revolution and the role of the media in underground culture. The mistake the *Argus* interviewer makes that seems to anger Kesey is the assumption that Kesey is *part* of the counterculture while Kesey seems to see himself, perhaps rightfully so, as being so important to the genesis of the American mid-century counterculture that he is actually *beyond* it. A watchmaker god, he has initiated actions but does not need to involve himself with the day-to-day drama or to use the right buzzwords. He is concerned with the future, not the present or the past. By the time of the 1992 interview with Todd Brendan Fahey, for instance, Kesey is re-inventing and demonstrating his relevance through his understanding of how newly developing media and technology were influencing writing overall: "the novel," he said to Fahey, "will sell as though it's a novel, but you'll play it through your video" (128).

Yet we also see in the interviews a man (rather than a legend) who moves from youth to old age to death, specifically fighting off the encroaching and debilitating conditions of diabetes, hepatitis C, and the after-effects of a stroke. In the later interviews, he is sometimes rueful about early life mistakes, questioning whether he is still relevant or how he can regain relevance in late middle age. He spends time recounting the physical strength of his youth, and readers watch as his political views towards issues like feminism and abortion shift as does the culture changes around him. By 1986 he tells KBOO radio, "I don't know if I've got another *Great Notion* in me . . . Maybe you can only do that at a certain time . . . we went through a period of time in which we were being taken by the muse without having to reflect. It was moving us" (105-6).

That change, revealing the struggle of a life lived, echoes throughout the interviews. For instance, Gordon Lish's 1963 interview with Kesey reveals the difficulty that the establishment had in placing Kesey in a literary school and Kesey's rejection of the concept of an artist portraying life as it is, that is, the difference between reportage and fiction. In this same interview, Kesey states that he does not see Kerouac as a novelist, but rather as a reporter (23). We also see here Kesey connecting his psychedelic experiments with the organizational strategy for *Sometimes a Great Notion* (1964). The drugs, he says, revealed to him "[p]oints of *view* and points of *time*. Whole bunches of ways of looking at the same event" (20). This revelation inspired the multiple points of view within *Sometimes a Great Notion*, but when he was interviewed by Pacifica Radio in 1965, a year after the publication of the text, Kesey expressed doubts about what was left to say in writing. He admitted believing that everything had been done before and feeling deeply the struggle to say something in a novel way. That struggle dogged him throughout the years. The 1986 interview with John Nance, Paul Pintarich, and Sharon Wood on KBOO radio is notable for Kesey's questioning of why American writers complete their best works in their youth and do not age into better work. Notable too is the fact that the writers who he lists as not improving with age—Fitzgerald, Hemingway, Faulkner, and Steinbeck—all struggled with substance abuse and addiction, a point to which Kesey, at least in this interview, seems blind.

While the strength of the collection lies in revelatory depictions such as these, the volume overall is somewhat uneven. Several of the interviews are extremely dated and remind the reader of just how long ago these interviews were recorded and how different the world now is. A prime example is the 1971 interview published in *The Realist* and conducted by fellow counterculture giant Paul Krassner. The concepts and the language Krassner and Kesey use to discuss them, such as "negative energy" and "women's lib," have changed or long since fallen into cliché. It is also in this interview that Kesey refers to abortion as "the worst worm in the revolutionary philosophy," although Krassner notes in the transcript that a "couple of years later" Kesey repudiated his original views on abortion to him in a private conversation (59).

There are some interviews in which these multiple streams of Kesey's life meet, and the collection is much better for it. For instance, in the 1990 interview with Carolyn Knox-Quinn from *College Composition and Communication*, Kesey, who in many of the prior interviews dwells on the importance of teachers in his writing career, takes on the role of instructor and explains, through reflection, how teaching a group of University of Oregon graduate students and the subsequent collaborative novel, *Caverns*, created in the class, influenced his own ideas about writing. He speaks in detail of the renewed energy he felt from writing and editing with his students. "You get tired of doing things by yourself . . . When you give something and the other person knows that he got it. That'll recharge you on both ends" (123).

Starting with the Knox-Quinn interview, we see a much changed Kesey, and by 1999, Robert Elder, in *Salon*, was able to suggest that Kesey, the last surviving member of "the pantheon of '60s counterculture icons," had become something of a spiritual relic (173). Like religious pilgrims, writers were compelled to sit next to and speak with this man who had seen and been the progenitor of so much of the literary counterculture that they had grown up taking for granted. Indeed, the final interview with Mike Finoia in *Relix* magazine is respectful reminiscence rather than revelation—a young man sitting with an old man and asking him what life was like in the old days.

Interviews in the collection include "Ken Kesey's first 'trip'," Menlo Park Veterans Hospital, 1959; "What the hell you looking in here for, Daisy Mae?," Gordon Lish, 1963; "Ken Kesey at N.D.E.A.," Pacifica Radio Archives, 1965; "The evening standard interview: Ken Kesey," Ray Connolly, 1969; "Once a great notion," *Ann Arbor Argus*, 1970; "An impolite interview," Paul Krassner, 1971; "Ken Kesey summing up the '60s, sizing up the '70s," Linda Gaboriau, 1972; "Ken Kesey: the prince of pranksters," Rick Saunders, Bob Nesbitt, and Vaughn Binzer, 1976; "Getting Better," John Nance, Paul Pintarich, and Sharon Wood, 1986; "The Fresh Air Interview: Ken Kesey," Terry Gross, 1989; "Collaboration in the writing classroom: an interview with Ken Kesey," Carolyn Knox-Quinn, 1990; "Comes spake the cuckoo," Todd Brendan Fahey, 1992; "Ken Kesey: Writing is an Act of Performance," Dan McCue, 1993; An Interview with Ken Kesey," Matthew Rick and Mary Jane Fenex, 1993; "Ken Kesey: The Art of Fiction no. 136," Robert Faggen, 1993; "Ken Kesey: Still on the Bus," Robert K. Elder, 1999; and "Ken Kesey's Last Interview," Mike Finoia, 1999.

—Michael J. Dittman, *Butler County Community College*

The Village: 400 Years of Beats and Bohemians, Radicals and
Rogues, a History of Greenwich Village
John Strausbaugh
(New York: Ecco/HarperCollins, 2013)

Among the strange details that emerged after Philip Seymour Hoffman's untimely death was the cost of his monthly rent for the apartment he occupied on Bethune Street, in the West Village, after separating from his partner and their children and leaving the $4.2 million Jane Street condominium they all shared. He paid $10,000 a month for his Greenwich Village apartment. By all accounts, Hoffman matched the Village's eclectic, bohemian feel as a screen and stage actor and as a financial supporter of the Labyrinth Theater, a Bank Street progressive performance space. His rent and mortgage, however, were hardly bohemian, and the details of his real estate possessions illustrate what the Village is today and what it takes to live there. Once a crucible of American culture—from bohemians to Beats to rockers—Greenwich Village is now a high-end real estate enclave, but its history and cultural impact form an invaluable legacy that John Strausbaugh captures effectively in *The Village: 400 Years of Beats and Bohemians, Radicals and Rogues, a History of Greenwich Village.*

Strausbaugh understands what rent means to neighborhoods in New York City. When he first arrived in the city in 1990 as the associate editor of *New York Press*, an independent, often-irreverent counterweight to the increasingly irrelevant *Village Voice*, he lived in Greenwich Village, but quickly moved to the East Village, where he found a taste of the old Village life, at least for a short period of time. Strausbaugh was a primary contributor and editor for *New York Press* from 1990-2002, and wrote for and hosted *The New York Times* "Weekend Explorer." He knows New York. Like the people he chronicles in *The Village*, Strausbaugh was attracted to the freedom from conformity the Village represented: "The artists, radicals, and misfits drawn to the Village for all those years were always a small and transient minority, though a highly visible and vocal one" (xi). The author of *Sissy Nation: How America Became a Culture of Wimps and Stoopits*, among other books, Strausbaugh clearly regrets the loss of what the old Village embodied. But he does not indulge in nostalgia, for he knows that freedom can lead to self-destruction and that booze, drugs, sex, and corruption are found in the same place as artistic and cultural freedom. "The history of Greenwich Village," he notes, "is littered with the corpses of those who drank themselves to creative ruin or death, overdosed on various drugs . . . or partied themselves into oblivion" (xi). *The Village* uses 624 pages to tell the Greenwich Village's social and cultural history in lively anecdotal fashion. The book is well researched, entertaining, and encyclopedic in scope, although it displays faults common to a journalistic writing style, especially in the final chapters of the book.

In the early twentieth century, Greenwich Village's attraction was cheap rent, which pulled creative people into what had once been a marshy landscape that indigenous people called Sapokanikan. In 1811, the so-called Randel Plan, named for its chief engineer, presented the grid of east-west streets and north-south avenues that defines modern-day Manhattan. The plan, according to Strausbaugh, served the desires of commercial real estate interests, except for a small slice of the West Side: "One small area on the map bucked the precision-tooled order. Just above Hudson Street on the Hudson flank of the island lay a maze of crooked, angled streets, a small eruption of eccentricity and disorder: the former *Bossen Bouwerie,* now called Greenwich Village" (8). This odd urban patchwork became a place for immigrants, creative artists, and transients. Greenwich Village, perhaps one of the most famous neighborhoods in the world, would become "the cultural capital of the Western world," particularly flourishing during the first seventy years of the twentieth century. "Abstract Expressionism, Off- and Off-Off-Broadway theater, bebop, the Beats, avant-garde filmmaking, the early glimmerings of the folk revival" all bloomed in and around the Village. Even John Lennon found freedom from celebrity there after the Beatles broke up. The Village became the epicenter of gay liberation in the 1970s and the AIDS epidemic in the 1980s. Its history illustrates how this small warren of streets continually reinvented itself while retaining its bohemian roots.

Like so many good New York reporters, Strausbaugh works best when he is dealing with narratives about people. He presents vagabonds, rogues, loafers, martyrs, and the famous who made the Village distinct: "The history of Greenwich Village, like the history of New York City as a whole, is fantastically deep, layered, fragmented, and fractal," he warns his readers (xiv). Using the voices and portraits of its residents, Strausbaugh chronicles how in 400 years the Village was transformed from a swampy field to a place where new mothers push strollers the size of Smart Cars.

After an informative introduction that describes the structure of his book, Strausbaugh starts at the beginning: the Dutch outpost called *Noortwyck,* marshland and woods that would become Greenwich Village. Wouter Van Twiller, the director-general of the Dutch settlement who succeeded Peter Minuit in 1633, established a tobacco farm on 200 acres of the property, which he called *Bossen Bouwerie* (Farm in the Woods) (4). In the 1630s, Van Twiller transferred two parcels of the plantation to Jan Van Rotterdam and Francis Lastley; the lane that divided "their farms would eventually come to be known as Christopher Street, the oldest street in the area" (4). Strausbaugh dedicates only about fifteen pages to the early history of the Village. Before the conclusion of the second chapter, he is already introducing Greenwich Village in the nineteenth century. At Chapter 3, "The First Bohemians,"

Strausbaugh is exploring Pfaff's basement tavern, the favorite drinking spot of New York's original bohemians, and he is firmly planted in nineteenth-century New York City. He describes Greenwich Village as an "engine of culture" fueled by people.

The Village contains four parts: 1) From the Beginning Through the "Golden Age," 2) The Dry Decade, the Red Decade, World War II, 3) The Greenwich Village Renaissance, and 4) The Last Hurrah. Each of the four sections focuses almost exclusively on the people who contributed to the literary, musical, and political culture of the twentieth-century Village. Some of their nineteenth-century ancestors remain important in the book, notably Edgar Allen Poe, who lived briefly on what is now West 3rd Street and on Waverly Place, and Walt Whitman, who frequented Pfaff's waiting for critical attention as a poet and seeking male companionship. While disputing Poe's "first bohemian" label—"he never flaunted his poverty" and "didn't loaf and carouse" but did work "himself to a nub" (23)—Strausbaugh celebrates Whitman as part of the Village's Bohemian clique: "He was attracted to Pfaff's—and to the attention its crowd was getting—at a time when he was avidly seeking attention for himself and for *Leaves of Grass*" (39). Occupying a small place in the raucous Pfaff's, perhaps meeting Fred Vaughan, the inspiration for his "Calamus" poems, there, Whitman personifies nineteenth-century bohemianism.

Whitman, of course, provides an ideal link between nineteenth-century bohemianism and many renowned twentieth-century writers. However, Strausbaugh also presents other twentieth-century literary figures who found their way to Greenwich Village but are now lost to time: Ada Clare, born Jane McElhenney in Charleston, South Carolina, a poet and actress who celebrated the fact that she had a child outside of wedlock; Henry Clapp Jr., who founded and edited the *Saturday Press*, a short-lived broadsheet best known for championing Whitman's *Leaves of Grass* and publishing Mark Twain's "Jim Smiley and his Jumping Frog"; Fitz-James O'Brien, an Irish writer who used both his wit and fists to make his points, reviewed theater for the *Saturday Press*, and wrote a "Man About Town" column for *Harper's*; and playwright, novelist, and artist Rosalyn Drexler, who performed on the professional women's wrestling circuit as Rosa Carlo, the Mexican Spitfire. Strausbaugh seems to enjoy writing about these marginalized Greenwich Village figures, for, although often neglected, they are colorful and original. He also celebrates the more well known Dawn Powell, who "held court from a corner table at Lafayette's Café, collecting the anecdotes, gossip, quips, and characters" that occupy her New York novels (149). *The Village* is ripe with characters like these—people who made Greenwich Village an essential place but whose contributions are not remembered.

As Strausbaugh expands his anecdotal biography of the Village, he exposes one of the book's most serious flaws. Unless one knows Greenwich Village well, it is difficult to follow the writer down the Village's crooked, cramped streets. Including a map for uninitiated readers would make it easier to follow Strausbaugh's pathways.

Courtesy of Google Maps

It is possible Strausbaugh wants his readers to explore the physical space of the Village on their own. The geographical boundaries of Greenwich Village have always been uncertain. In his essay "Rents Were Low in Greenwich Village," writer and editor Floyd Dell captured the various fluctuations of Greenwich Village's boundaries: "When I arrived in the Village [1913], its intelligentsia was socially dominant, social reform was its keynote, and it was expanding to take in Union Square" (261). In his introduction, Strausbaugh discusses the lack of agreement when it comes to defining the Village's borders. Most maps outline its boundaries with West 14th Street on the north, Broadway on the East, West Houston Street on the south, and the Hudson River on the west. According to Strausbaugh, the journalist and poet Djuna Barnes insisted that the Village went no further than West 12th Street to the north, but she believed that the southern border was the Battery, where "it commits suicide" (xiii). Before the 1970s, the area down to Canal Street on the Hudson side was considered the "south village" (xiii).

Its fuzzy geographic limits notwithstanding, Greenwich Village exerted an undeniable cultural power, equal to, according to Strausbaugh, Athens, Elizabethan London, Paris, and Berlin "for as long or longer than those fabled places" (ix). Strausbaugh backs up this ambitious claim not by breaking new ground but by transforming a collection of articles and profiles that have appeared in the *New*

York Press, *The New York Times*, the *Chiseler*, *Cabinet*, and the *Truth Barrier* into a rambling account of a mythic, reinvented, and reconstructed portion of Manhattan that still draws tourists and romantics, even though what they are looking for has moved to Brooklyn, Hoboken, and Jersey City. Strausbaugh explains how artists, scoundrels, immigrants, sexual adventurers, and workers of all kinds lived together until rents and gentrification exploded in the late 1980s and the 1990s. Village bohemians, artists, writers, musicians, and misfits clearly captured Strausbaugh's imagination. Why not? He has a galaxy of "stars" to work with: Hart Crane, Edmund Wilson, e.e. cummings, Willa Cather, John Reed, Henry Miller, James Agee, Djuna Barnes, John Dos Passos, Emma Goldman, Marianne Moore, Edna St. Vincent Millay, Eugene O'Neill, Dawn Powell, Thomas Wolf, Jimmy Walker, Margaret Sanger, Fiorello La Guardia, Edward Albee, Woody Guthrie, James Baldwin, Bob Dylan, Richard Wright, David Amran, Jack Kerouac, Gregory Corso, Frank O'Hara, Allen Ginsberg, Jane Jacobs, Ed Koch, and William S. Burroughs. And this list only touches a few of the figures Strausbaugh presents in *The Village*. After finishing *The Village*, browsing through the index in order to recall all the people who populated this small postage stamp of a place within New York City reveals the cultural currency Strausbaugh had to work with and underlines why Greenwich Village remains an essential part of our cultural history despite the commercial shift in the neighborhood since the 1990s.

For all the attention focused on celebrity figures, unfortunately, chapter 20, "The Beat Generation," and chapter 21, "Pull My Daisy," add little to Beat Studies scholarship. Each chapter recounts well-worn Beat history. Except for a reminder of the "druggy Fugazzi's on Sixth Avenue and the smoky, livelier, but still rough San Remo" and the role of Bill Cannastra, "the Beats' guide to the Remo scene," Strausbaugh reports on Beat culture rather than investigating it (297). He does reproduce a quote from journalist and novelist Pete Hamill's memoir *A Drinking Life,* which serves as a reminder of how the Village drew disparate people together. Hamill attended one of Kerouac's short readings between jazz sets at Max Gordon's Village Vanguard. Later at the Cedar Tavern, Hamill saw Kerouac and his friends near the bar: "I said hello. He looked at me in a suspicious way and nodded." Kerouac bought drinks for all his crowd, "always polite, but his eyes scared, a twitch in his face and a sour smell coming off him . . . The painters gave him a who-the-fuck-is-this-guy? look" (306). Hamill, still drinking at that time and an emerging journalistic voice, could not acknowledge Kerouac's importance. By the late 1950s, the Bleecker-MacDougal area became a draw for beatniks and tourists looking for Beats. A few weeks after shooting *Pull My Daisy* (1959), David Amram and Kerouac entered the Figaro, a café where their photographs adorned the walls: "It's a new scene, the manager explained to them. The fun times are over. Business is booming all over the Village…They all get dressed up and come down to the

Village to be Beatniks...You guys started a trend" (315). Strausbaugh concludes Chapter 21 with Kerouac's sad death in Florida in front of a television set, a reminder of the sometimes-extreme cost of creative freedom.

When Strausbaugh presents a particular chapter he is invested in, his voice is crisp and compelling, providing more than a journalistic take on the subject. At other points, though, he moves too quickly through information, which creates an imbalance between chapters. He also makes small errors that could come from journalistic deadline demands. David Amram is featured in multiple places in *The Village,* and it is evident that he and Strausbaugh have spent a great deal of time together. Yet when discussing Barry Farber, the politically conservative, long serving New York radio talk-show host, Strausbaugh writes, "David Amram, who feels a kinship with Faber as a fellow Jew with southern roots in the biggest of northern cities, says he always admired Faber's courage and conviction" (320). However, Amram was born in Philadelphia, spent time in Washington, DC, and has lived in New York City for the majority of his life—he was not a southerner. In Chapter 24, Strausbaugh identifies "the tiny village of Endicott in western New York" as the home of Haralambos Monroe ("Harry") Koutoukas, an early Off-Off Broadway actor and writer. However, Endicott, which lies on the Southern Tier of New York State, used to be the home of IBM's manufacturing center and is a midsized industrial city, not a tiny village.

While these errors are small, they are possibly the result of taking on an ambitious subject like the history of Greenwich Village. Clearly, Strausbaugh struggled to include everything he believed necessary to capture the Village's history. As his book reaches its conclusion, Strausbaugh relies on shorter chapters. For example, he uses eight pages to discuss Lenny Bruce and Valerie Solanas, two figures who deserve more exposition. Strausbaugh links Bruce with Howard and Ella Solomon's Café Au Go Go, a Persian-themed Village coffee house that would become one of the most well known music clubs in the city. In one week, Bruce was arrested twice on obscenity charges at the Au Go Go, primarily because he claimed Jackie Kennedy was trying to "save her ass" after her husband was shot in Dallas, Texas (421). The second time, Howard Solomon was arrested along with Bruce. As Strausbaugh notes, Bruce "represented a rebellion against sexual repression...Like the Beats, he loved jazz, spontaneous riffing, and lots of drugs...and he startled the government into hostile reaction" (419). Bruce advocated for free speech, battled with the FBI, defended himself against obscenity charges in court, and challenged conventional sources of power. Strausbaugh's account, though brief, explains why Bruce ran into so much trouble in Greenwich Village—the city wanted to clean up in advance of the 1964 World's Fair. Ginsberg worked to help Bruce, asking many Village luminaries to sign a "petition against his censorship [and] harassment" (421). Kerouac, we are told, refused to sign. Bruce never recovered, losing his cabaret card, ending his career in New York City. Because Bruce is a fascinating subject and because of the information Strausbaugh reports in a few pages, a more detailed account of Bruce's connection with Greenwich Village would have bolstered this portion of the chapter.

Likewise, his reporting on Valerie Solanas, perhaps most famous as the woman who shot Andy Warhol, is strong but limited. According to Strausbaugh, "like Djuna Barnes decades earlier [Solanas] was quite damaged" by the time she reached the Village (426). The victim of a difficult life, Solanas was 30 years old when she reached the Village, seeking to become a writer but still turning tricks and bumming spare change to get by. The February 9, 1967, issue of *The Village Voice* featured two ads Solanas placed. One was for readings at the Directors Theater School on East 14th Street of her play *Up Your Ass or From the Cradle or The Big Suck or Up From the Slime*. The second ad was for her *SCUM Manifesto*, available for $1.50 at the 8th Street Bookstore (427). Strausbaugh suggests that both the manifesto and the play "can be seen as early examples of the extremist feminist-separatist tracts that became more familiar in the 1970s" (428). Further, he sees the manifesto as a "distant cousin to William [S.] Burroughs's mad sci-fi visions" (428). Bookended by the Bruce and Solanas sketches, Strausbaugh inserts a brief commentary indicating that by the mid-1960s the Village was no longer a sanctuary for outsiders. However, he does not connect this observation to Lenny Bruce or Valerie Solanas. At times, Chapter 27, "Lenny Bruce and Valerie Solanas," seems better suited as a newspaper or magazine article. Yet some of the material contained in the chapter is fascinating and matches well with the Village culture he has laid out up until this point in his appraisal of the neighborhood's history. While neither Bruce nor Solanas had a large impact on the history of Greenwich Village, they both possessed Village sensibilities—roguish, radical, self-destructive, and misunderstood.

Still, Strausbaugh's writing is strong and informative in most chapters, even his brief ones, and he can present a great deal of information that contributes to the history of Greenwich Village in a few pages. For example, he recounts in solid detail the history of America's first black professional theater company, African Grove, located at the corner of Bleeker and Mercer Streets and founded in Greenwich Village in 1821 by William Henry Brown. Strausbaugh observes, "The seating policy at the African Grove, amazingly, instituted reverse segregation: whites were relegated to the back rows, because, as a handbill stated, they don't know how to conduct themselves at entertainments for ladies and gentlemen of color" (66). He continues with the observation that the Village became a small zone "[w]ith its jazz clubs and its bohemian and progressive residents…where blacks and whites met and mingled more freely than in most of the rest of the country—not a paradise of racial equality, maybe, but certainly ahead of the national curve on matters of race" (73). Strausbaugh is not concerned with theoretical analysis; rather, his research is sound and his writing style straightforward, delivered with a journalist's eye for intriguing narratives, unique places, and original people.

Of course, in Greenwich Village, Strausbaugh has an expansive and rich subject, which cannot easily be contained in a 600-page book. He concludes *The Village* with the aftermath of the AIDS epidemic: "Plague [the epidemic of 1798] had played a significant role in the development of Greenwich Village in the early nineteenth century. Now another plague contributed to its transformation at the end of the twentieth" (545). While Strausbaugh makes it evident that he believes the Village is no longer the "engine of culture," for almost seven decades in the twentieth century its cultural significance cannot be ignored. The book's Epilogue, which caps this massive effort to represent a place, an atmosphere, and a sociocultural mecca, begins with Marky Iannello, an Italian working class man Strausbaugh abruptly dropped into Chapter 23, "Standing Up to Moses and the Machine," which revolves around Jane Jacobs's defense of the Village against Robert Moses, the "master builder" of metropolitan New York. Iannello sums up the contemporary Village for Strausbaugh: "The Village is full of people who are not from New York, who don't give a shit about New York, who are only here to make money" (546). Or as a protest postcard once popular in the Village put it: "More Jane Jacobs, Less Marc Jacobs" (550). However, change is inevitable, especially in New York City. Philip Seymour Hoffman's Bethune Street apartment, described as a "quintessential Village home," was leased for $10,500 48 hours after it was placed on the market—a $500 rent increase.

From Strausbaugh's perspective, the Village as a refuge for outsiders has ended: "The Village that had been a rare sanctuary in the 1950s was now just one node in a international chain of countercultural centers that included every decent-sized city and college campus" (423). Yet, in his book, Strausbaugh is able to capture the spirit of this neighborhood of dreams and dreamers. He uses a vivid journalistic style, captivating street perspectives, and dedicated research. No matter who lives there now, the portion of Manhattan known as the Village will always remain historically significant. Its flaws notwithstanding, *The Village: 400 Years of Beats and Bohemians, Radicals and Rogues, a History of Greenwich Village* is an excellent addition to the history of New York City, Greenwich Village, and the fuel flowing into and out of America's "engine of culture."

—Jack Ryan, *Gettysburg College*

Works Cited

Dell, Floyd. "Rents Were Low in Greenwich Village." *The Greenwich Village Reader: Fiction, Poetry, and Reminiscences.* Ed. June Skinner Sawyers. New York: Cooper Square Press, 2001. 257-266. Print.

Call Me Burroughs: A Life
Barry Miles
(New York: Twelve Books, 2013)

Barry Miles has written a landmark biography of William S. Burroughs; it will no doubt become an important reference for scholars and critics for a long time. A factually detailed narrative—perhaps overwhelmingly so at 718 pages—the book pulls together an impressive array of research and sources. One of Miles's most important sources is the extensive research on Burroughs's childhood and young adulthood, undertaken by James Grauerholz, Burroughs's companion and agent from 1974 until Burroughs's death in 1997 and his literary executor.[1] Miles also makes extensive use of Ted Morgan's taped interviews for his 1988 biography of Burroughs,[2] and he relies on Rob Johnson's research on Burroughs's "lost" years in Texas in the late '40s and Stewart Meyers's unpublished journals of his friendship with Burroughs during "the Bunker years" in New York in the '70s. Miles was himself an important figure in London in the '60s as co-owner of the Indica bookstore/gallery and co-founder of the underground magazine *International Times* which published Burroughs. Thus, he knew Burroughs and many of his friends from 1965 on and conducted many interviews over time. As a writer and researcher, he is well-qualified as Burroughs's chronicler, having previously published biographies of Ginsberg, Kerouac, and Burroughs himself (his 1993 biography is a brief "portrait"), as well as a book about the Beat Hotel where Burroughs and Brion Gysin began their cut-up experiments. He also catalogued the Burroughs/Gysin archives in 1972 prior to the sale to a private collector and subsequently published a Burroughs bibliography. During his work on the archives, Miles discovered the missing manuscript of *Queer*. He co-edited with Grauerholz the restored text edition of *Naked Lunch* in 2001. His research and organizational skills are evident not only in the complex weaving of a broad range of sources into the chronological narrative, but also in the excellent bibliography organized by topic and the equally thorough index, which can be profitably read in and of itself.

Although Miles's earlier biography of Burroughs was a portrait of an icon, *Call Me Burroughs* could be seen as debunking the legend that has been so much a part of Burroughs's career. As Miles told Davis Schneiderman, "having known Bill for 30+ years and now spent years studying his life and work, I obviously no longer have that adolescent romantic view of him as the tortured bohemian artist. I know too much about him, and have witnessed too much of his home life to project onto him any more." In his interview with Oliver Harris, he stated that his goal as a biographer was to establish as many facts as possible for the next generation of scholars and readers.

This he has done. However, although the book is clearly structured and the writing style presents no difficulties, many will find the massive accumulation of details tedious to read. Yet this factual density successfully punctures the glamorous aura that made Burroughs a fascinating figure associated with '50s cool, '60s rebellion, '70s punk, and '80s postmodernism. *Call Me Burroughs* is a thorough, traditional biography, which will be of interest to scholars, but it is not a book for fans.

Given the size and scope of this biography, one question to ask from a scholarly point of view is "What do we learn that is new about Burroughs's life and work?" This review will focus on a few topics that contribute new knowledge or new details which alter our perspective on the man and his work. *Call Me Burroughs* begins with revelations: the early chapters plunge us into a wealth of information about Burroughs's childhood, and this is indeed an important contribution because Burroughs was always reticent about his early life and his family, never divulging many details and expressing annoyance at the suggestion that his parents were wealthy or that he had received income from a trust fund (mentioned in Kerouac's fictionalized portrayals and taken as fact by some early critics). Miles's narrative (based on Grauerholz's research) describes a privileged *haute bourgeois* upbringing that included servants, private schools, residence in an elite neighborhood, expensive automobiles, summers on Lake Huron, family trips to Europe, and the assumption that sons will go to Harvard. His material and social circumstances were no different from others of his class. Far from being isolated (as he implied in interviews and his fiction), Burroughs grew up within a substantial social network of family and friends; in fact, many men he met in childhood and later at Harvard remained lifelong friends and acquaintances. A similar picture of Burroughs's upper-middle class environment and circle of St. Louis friends is provided by Dusty Griffin in his recently published essay about Burroughs, Kammerer, and Carr.

Miles provides exact details about the family finances which should settle the matter of wealth once and for all. Burroughs's father, Mortimer Burroughs, inherited shares in the Burroughs company which he sold for $100,000 (equal to $2.8 million in 2012 according to Miles). He kept back a few shares which he sold just before the 1929 crash for $276,000 ($3.6 million in 2012 dollars). He owned and operated a profitable glass company for many years, and later he and his wife owned garden and gift shops in St. Louis and Palm Beach, Florida. After Burroughs's graduation from college, his parents put him on an allowance of about $200 per month. At his mother's death, Burroughs inherited $10,000.[3]

Burroughs's parents provided a stable, caring home environment. Burroughs was very close to his mother who favored him over his brother, believing he had exceptional abilities. Miles says "it was a relationship out of Proust" and describes their shared interest in visions, dreams, magic, and the occult which occupied Burroughs his entire life (21). Given Burroughs's reticence about his childhood and his misogynistic declarations as an adult, his mother's influence has been largely overlooked. His father, although not demonstrative, was also supportive. His parents always bailed him out of trouble as a young adult, paid for psychiatric care and addiction cures, sent him an allowance until he was finally able to support himself (at the age of 50), and brought up his son—all without harsh reproach. Although not a "trust fund baby," Burroughs had a family safety net to rely on, and in his early adulthood, he exhibited a sometimes dangerous immaturity and irresponsibility that Rob Johnson portrayed in *The Lost Years*.

Miles's in-depth chronicle of Burroughs's early life also weaves in references to the heretofore unknown numerous appearances of the people and places of his youth throughout Burroughs's work—this discovery again the result of Grauerholz's research. The listing of these autobiographical elements foregrounds how much of Burroughs's fiction is the product of memory, reverie, and dreams, as well as fantasy. This new information will certainly alter future scholarship on Burroughs's life and work and will require new ways of thinking about autobiography and his experimental fiction.

The biography also reveals that, in spite of his denigration of Freud in his work from the '60s on, Burroughs spent years in psychoanalysis, first encouraged by his parents and later pursued on his own. After rejecting psychoanalysis, he turned to self-analysis and self-help techniques—most notably cut-ups and Scientology. It was Brion Gysin who persuaded him that psychoanalysis was worthless and introduced him to Scientology, cut-ups, and magic as alternative forms of psychic exploration. One can draw the conclusion that Burroughs felt that something was wrong and was seeking insight or relief from mental anguish. Psychoanalysis focused on a traumatic childhood incident of a sexual nature involving his nanny, which Burroughs believed had blighted his sexuality, but years of analysis never clarified exactly what had happened and led to no resolution. Miles uncovers intriguing circumstantial detail on what may have occurred along with traces of it in the fiction. Surprisingly, he does not allude to any research on childhood sexual abuse and its long-term effects.

Contributing to his psychic unease was Burroughs's struggle with his sexuality, and Miles provides intimate information on his sexual relationships—both physically and emotionally—presenting a picture of lifelong disappointment. It was not easy to be gay in the era in which Burroughs grew up; the opprobrium made him fearful of exposure and ridicule. He was shy and sensitive and ambivalent about his sexuality for many years, and he was a vulnerable sex partner except when he was paying for it—even then he could be the object of contempt. All of his most serious relationships with other men ended in rejection. Because he knew Burroughs personally from 1965 on, Miles is in a position to provide insight unavailable to most biographers, especially about Burroughs's long-term relationship with Ian Sommerville. In addition, there was a lifetime of guilt to carry after shooting his wife, Joan, in a drunken game of William Tell and regret for his inability to establish a paternal relationship with his son who destroyed himself with alcohol. His failed relationships led Miles to state in his final chapter that Burroughs had had an unhappy life: "he was plagued by loneliness and lack of love, racked with guilt, not just over the death of Joan, but for the neglect of friends and family" (633).

Gysin gave Burroughs a new explanation for psychic dysfunction: the Ugly Spirit, a demonic external force that had invaded Burroughs early in life and later supposedly caused him to shoot his wife. (The Ugly Spirit was revealed to Gysin during experiments with magic and cut-ups.) As with Gysin's other ideas, Burroughs made the Ugly Spirit an important part of his world view and his fiction; he stopped looking within for Freudian sources of neurosis and instead explored ways to identify and struggle against an evil spirit that he thought had poisoned his life.[4] He threw himself obsessively into cut-up experiments in various media and Scientology. Although Miles takes a common-sense approach to the death of Joan, stating that it was basically the result of a drunk with a gun, he seems to accept the Ugly Spirit as some kind of explanation for Burroughs's psychic wound. He introduces *Call Me Burroughs* with a chapter about Burroughs's participation in an exorcism conducted by a Navajo shaman in 1992, stating that "this [biography] is the story of William Burroughs' battle with the Ugly Spirit" (6).[5] Miles never analyzes the meaning of this idea, but merely quotes what Burroughs has said about it at different times. Although the Ugly Spirit is effective in the fiction as a malevolent force, a spirit or metaphor is not very convincing as the key to Burroughs's life. The exorcism does show that Burroughs was still seeking solace in later years, but this form of therapy was only the latest in a series of unconventional, magical techniques he had explored, and, as often in the past, was suggested by friends in his current social milieu.

We also learn that, in spite of repeated attempts to break his habit and in spite of telling interviewers over the years that opiates impeded creativity, Burroughs was in fact a lifelong addict, and pretty much all of his fiction was written under the influence of drugs—mainly heroin and marijuana.[6] Burroughs told Ted Morgan that he found marijuana an aid to writing: "I smoke pot in the afternoon for work. If I can get it, it makes all the difference. It's just that extra spark" (611). Although often ambivalent about his drug use, at the end of his life Burroughs said that becoming a junky was the best thing he ever did because addiction, the world of junk and its underworld characters, provided an important subject for his writing (633). As he stated early on in *Junky*, junk gives the addict a special angle of vision: "you see things different when you return from junk" (127-28). Miles concludes that "the role of drugs in Burroughs' life cannot be overemphasized," and "no one has yet done a serious study of what must surely be the biggest influence of all upon his work: the different drugs he was taking when he wrote his books" (633).

Miles's detailed descriptions of the writing, compiling, editing, and publishing of Burroughs's work shows as never before the extent of Burroughs's artistic collaborations—that his major work would never have been completed or published without the assistance of others, and that Burroughs actively sought and acted upon editorial advice. Allen Ginsberg was central in organizing the materials and arranging publication of *Junky, The Yage Letters*, and *Naked Lunch*. The latter was typed and edited by several friends in Tangier and Paris (who found some of its pages scattered around the floor): Alan Ansen, Jack Kerouac, Ginsberg, Brion Gysin, and Sinclair Beiles. Ginsberg played the major editorial role, since many sections of *Naked Lunch* were first included in letters to Ginsberg that he saved, and since he helped to compile the manuscript in both Tangier and Paris. When Burroughs's publisher was pressing for the final version, Gysin and Beiles determined the final order of the material with little input from Burroughs. *The Soft Machine* was assembled and edited by Ginsberg and Gysin in Paris while Burroughs was in Tangier. Sommerville made important contributions to *The Ticket That Exploded* and *Nova Express*, partly based on tape recorder experiments, which Burroughs could not have done without him. Grauerholz played a significant role in organizing and editing the final trilogy, *Cities of the Red Night*, *The Place of Dead Roads*, and *The Western Lands*. Richard Seaver, Burroughs's U.S. editor for 25 years, had input as well. Of course, Burroughs's multimedia experiments in the '60s were all collaborative efforts with Gysin, Sommerville, and Antony Balch; and Grauerholz orchestrated his readings, appearances, and recordings after his return to the U.S. in 1974. Burroughs praised "the third mind" that arises from collaboration and always gave credit to his collaborators, yet critics rarely write in depth about Burroughs's work as a product of collaboration or the collaborative process.

Call Me Burroughs is not a critical biography, nor does Miles devote any attention to what critics have said—how Burroughs's writing has been received and assessed. He seems determined to ignore any academic criticism, occasionally alluding to scholarly commentary only to dismiss it. Discussion of the works is limited to citation of biographical and (some) literary sources. This approach to the fiction seems almost a throwback to what was a common mode of literary criticism in the early part of the twentieth century. The biographical references will be valuable for future critics but are often employed by Miles reductively. *Junky, Queer*, and *The Yage Letttters* are read as autobiography, not as fictionalized narratives. *Naked Lunch* is said to be a picaresque novel (noting a few historical examples) with characters based on people and experiences in Tangier and Lee the narrator based on Burroughs himself. The celebrated "talking asshole" routine is about Burroughs's rejected desire for Ginsberg, just as *Queer* is the story of Burroughs's love affair with Lewis Marker. As the biography progresses, summaries of the works become briefer and even less useful. Post-*Naked Lunch* work is not really amenable to summary, but Miles does not turn to other ways of describing the later books. Miles does review Burroughs's influence as a writer and multi-media artist in his final chapter, but this consists of merely cataloguing his direct, acknowledged influence on particular writers, musicians, and filmmakers with no critical commentary.

Miles's nonjudgmental, "just the facts" approach to Burroughs's life is effective in producing a narrative that avoids sensationalizing and mythologizing, and in portraying the man at different ages and in different social settings, but he fails to convey why Burroughs is important as an writer/artist, why he has been so influential. The facts about Burroughs's reception are missing. Clearly, Miles decided that his own critical judgments were not relevant to his purpose, but he could have discussed the critical response of others, as John Geiger did very effectively in his biography of Gysin. In his interview with Harris, Miles stated that Burroughs's importance for him and for future generations is political, that his opposition to systems of control is even more relevant in our era of the expanded surveillance state. He does touch on this thesis in his conclusion, but again with no depth of analysis.

On the other hand, Miles's chronological, step-by-step narrative of materials, procedures, and technique is helpful in his discussion of Burroughs as a visual artist. He has the advantage of writing several years after Burroughs's death so that he can survey the paintings within the context of the whole body of his work. He gives a good overview of Burroughs's evolution as an artist, beginning with early cutups, photographic collages, and scrapbooks in the '60s and shows the connection to the later paintings. Like the cut-ups, Burroughs's paintings began accidentally (with shotgun paintings); then, as Burroughs progressed with those experiments, he combined random effects with controlled selection and collage. First, he tried every possible way of shooting paint onto wood. He then turned to painting on paper, combining random marks with spray-painting around stencils or found objects and collage, then looking for images to photograph and re-use. Like the early collages, Burroughs's paintings are, according to Miles, an "assemblage of memories, personal references, and ideas suggested by random gestures and events, and are a snapshot of that moment of time" (598). Burroughs himself saw the paintings as "ports of entry" to another world of spirits, the magical universe that occupied him in his final trilogy. Miles skillfully traces the aesthetic continuity between the writing and the painting.

Based on extensive research, Miles's biography is a comprehensive, well-organized chronicle of Burroughs's life and career, and much can be gleaned from this biography about Burroughs's family and friends, his education and reading, his social and artistic circles, his many crackpot ideas and enthusiasms, all of the places that he lived and his living arrangements, his finances, his sexuality and sex partners, his cats, his guns, his clothes, his food, his death and burial, and more. Miles fulfills his stated goal of establishing the facts as thoroughly as possible for the next generation—a valid purpose since many facts have not been known or are obscured by legend. Nevertheless, the dense accumulation of detail without a critical perspective makes the book laborious to read and leaves the reader longing for an analysis of Burroughs's personality and more interpretation of the fiction. The Ugly Spirit fails to provide a convincing frame for an unhappy life and does little to explain how powerful works of art came into being or why they mean so much to others. *Call Me Burroughs* is a significant achievement but not the last word: it provides an impressive foundation for a future critical biography and for interpretation of Burroughs's work based on a fuller understanding of his life and creative process.

—Jennie Skerl, (retired) *West Chester University*

Notes

[1] James Grauerholz planned to write a biography of Burroughs and did extensive research from 1999 to 2010, gathering information on Burroughs's family, childhood, and young adulthood. He also researched the death of Joan Vollmer Burroughs. In addition, he is the person who knew Burroughs best at the end of his life in Lawrence, Kansas. When Grauerholz found he was unable to complete the biography, he invited Miles to take on the project.

[2] Ted Morgan taped over 100 hours of interviews with Burroughs over a period of four years for his 1988 biography, *Literary Outlaw*. The tapes were acquired by Arizona State University and subsequently transcribed by Miles.

[3] Miles also provides details on Burroughs's income from his books and his financial status throughout his career.

[4] The importance of Brion Gysin for Burroughs's work after *Naked Lunch* cannot be overestimated. He introduced Burroughs to key ideas and myths that appear in the fiction, and to cut-ups and the European avant-garde, taking him in a new artistic direction. After Gysin's death, his style of painting influenced Burroughs's paintings. Burroughs commented on Gysin's importance in his life and art many times, saying he was "the only man I've ever respected" (*Call Me Burroughs* 587). Geiger's biography of Gysin gives a thorough accounting of the Burroughs/Gysin collaborations.

[5] Miles has given credence to the Ugly Spirit for a long time, concluding his previous biography with the exorcism by the shaman.

[6] Burroughs was on a methadone maintenance program from 1980 on.

Works Cited

Burroughs, William S. *Cities of the Red Night*. New York: Holt, 1981. Print.
—. *Junky: The Definitive Text of Junk*. Ed. Oliver Harris. New York: Penguin, 2003. Print.
—. *Naked Lunch: The Restored Text*. Ed. James Grauerholz and Barry Miles. New York: Grove, 2001. Print.
—. *Nova Express: The Restored Text*. Ed. Oliver Harris. New York: Grove, 2014. Print.
—. *The Place of Dead Roads*. New York: Holt, 1983. Print.
—. *Queer: 25th Anniversary Edition*. Ed. Oliver Harris. New York: New York: Penguin, 2010. Print.
—. *The Soft Machine: The Restored Text*. Ed. Oliver Harris. New York: Grove, 2014. Print.
—. *The Ticket That Exploded: The Restored Text*. Ed. Oliver Harris. New York: Grove, 2014. Print.
—. *The Western Lands*. New York: Viking, 1987. Print.
Burroughs, William S. and Allen Ginsberg. *The Yage Letters Redux*. Ed. Oliver Harris. San Francisco: City Lights, 2006. Print.
Geiger, John. *Nothing is True Everything is Permitted: The Life of Brion Gysin*. New York: Disinformation, 2005. Print.
Griffin, Dusty. "The St. Louis Clique: Burroughs, Kammerer, and Carr." *Journal of Beat Studies 3* (2014): 1-45.
Johnson, Rob. *The Lost Years of William S. Burroughs: Beats in South Texas*. College Station: Texas A&M University Press, 2006. Print.
Miles, Barry. "Barry Miles in Conversation with Oliver Harris." William S. Burroughs Centennial Conference, Center for the Humanities, City University of New York, 25 Apr. 2014. Web. 15 June 2104.
—. *The Beat Hotel: Ginsberg, Burroughs, and Corso in Paris, 1957-1963*. New York: Grove, 2000. Print.
—. "Call Me (William Burroughs): A Conversation with Barry Miles." Interview by Davis Schneiderman. *The Huffington Post*, 13 Feb. 2014. Web.15 June 2014.
—. *Ginsberg: A Biography*. New York: Simon and Schuster, 1989. Print.
—. *Jack Kerouac, King of the Beats: A Portrait*. New York: Holt, 1998. Print.
—. *William Burroughs, El Hombre Invisible: A Portrait*. New York: Hyperion, 1993. Print.
Miles, Barry and Joe Maynard. *William S. Burroughs: A Bibliography, 1953-1973*. Charlottesville: U of Virginia, 1978. Print.
Morgan, Ted. *Literary Outlaw: The Life and Times of William S. Burroughs*. New York: Holt, 1988. Print.

The Soft Machine: The Restored Text
William S. Burroughs, edited and with an introduction by
Oliver Harris
(New York: Grove Press, 2014)

The Ticket That Exploded: The Restored Text
William S. Burroughs, edited and with an introduction by
Oliver Harris
(New York: Grove Press, 2014)

Nova Express: The Restored Text
William S. Burroughs, edited and with an introduction by
Oliver Harris
(New York: Grove Press, 2014)

A few years ago, I compared line-by-line a copy of the Olympia Press edition of William S. Burroughs's *The Ticket That Exploded* (1962) and a copy of the Grove Press *Ticket* (1967). I felt like a philologist comparing manuscripts as I noted the extensive differences between the two editions and wondered why critics so infrequently addressed changes that seemed significant to me. For example, Burroughs added more than fifty pages to the second edition of *Ticket*, and more than half of the first fifty-two pages are new. This striking critical lacuna extends to the other volumes of Burroughs's cut-up, or Nova, trilogy, and suggests a curious ambivalence towards their composition and publishing history, as if sensitivity to the manuscript changes of Burroughs's work would jeopardize appreciation of Burroughs's deliberately fragmented writing. As Michael Sean Bolton argues in his recent book *Mosaic of Juxtaposition: William S. Burroughs' Narrative Revolution*, a linear approach "toward the author's own intellectual and aesthetic development over time [would] interfere with the direct apprehension of Burroughs' work as it was crafted" (14). Even biographies of Burroughs give very little information about the complex publishing history of the cut-up trilogy. Surely a greater awareness of the historical context for the evolution of Burroughs's thought over years of composition would deepen and enrich our readings of his mysterious works and their relation to each other.

For the first time, Burroughs scholars now have access to the manuscript and publishing history of Burroughs's cut-up trilogy without having to consult many different archives and manuscripts. Oliver Harris's new editions of *The Soft Machine, The Ticket That Exploded*, and *Nova Express* will revolutionize the field of criticism on Burroughs's experimental writing. Thanks to Harris's formidable research and editing, scholars can now appraise these works within a broad, synthetic history of composition, manuscript revisions, and publication. Harris's painstaking, heroic editorial work draws on thousands of pages of archival material, from first drafts and variant typescripts to final long galleys. In the fascinating and detailed introductions to each volume, Harris offers valuable historical contexts and publishing histories. He situates the three books within Burroughs's creative work in four media: writing, audiotape, film, and artwork. The extensive notes to each edition identify all the cuts and insertions and editorial changes of the various editions of these works, as well as present significant selections from major archival variants. We can now trace against a larger background of manuscript sequence how Burroughs revised these works. Burroughs's experimental methods and source materials, formatting, punctuation, his choice of dashes and decisions about capitalization, all receive careful attention here.

Harris's meticulous research demonstrates the value of genetic readings as it puts to rest a number of myths about Burroughs's creative process. The very term "cut-up trilogy" is misleading. According to Harris, Burroughs never once referred to the "cut-up trilogy" in the '60s. His only reference to a trilogy, in 1962, was to *Naked Lunch*, *The Soft Machine*, and *Nova Express*. Only *The Soft Machine* is a "pure" cut-up work—by the time Burroughs started composing the following two volumes, he increasingly used the fold-in technique. The standard publication dates used by critics are based on the initial publication of these works: *The Soft Machine*, Olympia Press, 1961; *The Ticket That Exploded*, Olympia Press, 1962; *Nova Express*, Grove Press, 1964. However, the actual publication history is more complex than that: *The Soft Machine* (1961, 1966, 1968), *The Ticket That Exploded* (1962, 1967), and *Nova Express* (1964). Critics almost always work with the final published version of each text, but there are crucial differences among all the editions. Harris demonstrates how *Nova Express*, usually assumed to be the only unrevised work in the trilogy, was written and rewritten over three years and is actually a composite text based on the three major stages of its composition. Even more important, Harris's new edition emphasizes the significance of the composition history of the trilogy, which does not correspond to its publication history. Almost all of *Nova Express* was written months before Burroughs even started writing *The Ticket That Exploded*, but Burroughs's fast writing of *Ticket* and delays at Grove Press caused *Ticket* to be published almost two years before *Nova*. Reading the trilogy in the order of composition—*Soft Machine, Nova Express*, and *Ticket*—resolves the apparent contradiction noted by Timothy Murphy when he mentions how "although *The Ticket That Exploded* is only the second book of the trilogy, both Ginsberg and Burroughs agree that it actually 'brought it all to a climax' through 'the action of the Nova or of the explosion itself, by dissolving everything into a vibrating, soundless hum'" (244-45). Murphy explains this paradox of two conclusions as part of Burroughs's anti-narrative strategy through the use of cut-ups and argues, "it would be inconsistent to reinscribe that linear logic at a higher level by subordinating the cut-ups' rupture to traditional narrative structure—in other words, to arrange the trilogy itself in linear order" (138). However, the actual manuscript history offers a different perspective on the ending of *Ticket*. As Harris explains, "In the chronology of composition, it is *The Ticket* that 'repeats' *Nova Express*" (*Ticket* 249).

Another illusion Harris debunks with his prodigious feat of editing, as he presents the composition history, is the myth that the trilogy was simply drawn from a thousand-page *Naked Lunch* word hoard. The evidence of hundreds of archival draft pages reveals Burroughs as neither careless, haphazard nor drug-inspired in his revisions. Archival evidence confirms the radical impact of chance in his creative process, but also shows Burroughs to be a rigorous corrector of final drafts. One of the most revealing findings contradicts the received idea that the majority of Burroughs's revisions for later editions of the trilogy substituted narrative for cut-up material. For the second edition of *The Soft Machine*, for example, most of the narrative actually came from the first edition and the majority of cut-up material is new. Of roughly 10,000 words of cut-up material in the 1966 edition, only about a third came from the 1961 text.

As an example of the critical insights that can be generated through genetic readings, Harris shows through the manuscript history of the opening of *Nova Express* that the chapter "Last Words" was a last-minute addition to Burroughs's first draft manuscript. Harris cites a letter from Burroughs to his Grove Press publisher Barney Rosset that describes the section as mescaline-inspired and asks if it could be published in Grove's forthcoming edition of *Naked Lunch* (*Nova* 193). As Harris demonstrates, before this chapter became part of *Nova Express*, it appeared complete in *Evergreen Review*, partially in *The Yage Letters*, and had been proposed as a part of the Grove Press *Naked Lunch* and *The Exterminator*. Harris also discusses variant early drafts of "Last Words" that identify "Mr. K" with "Mr. Krushev," (sic) drafts that include "racist and sexist invective, signs of an ugly anti-semitism and misogyny that went unchecked during Burroughs's early messianic period" (*Nova* 194). Some of these references were edited out later and others were addressed openly in revisions, when Burroughs would identify everyone as victims of an anti-human conspiracy. As Harris demonstrates, the early "alternative, overlapping and expanded drafts…reveal the specifically political investment of Burroughs with the text" (*Nova* 195).

In a discussion of the textual and publication history of the chapter "Gongs of Violence" in *The Soft Machine*, Harris shows how one paragraph in the 1966 edition of the work can be related to two magazine texts, the 1968 edition of the book, an abandoned cut-up novel (*The Ugly Spirit*), and *Nova Express*. According to Harris, the most significant part of this complex publication history appears only in the 1965 Grove Press edition and the 1962 manuscript. Burroughs cut an entire chapter called "Male Image Back In" from the 1965 galleys. Harris chooses to include this particular version in his new edition because "its structure works more naturally with the organization of the 1966 text" (*Soft* 259-60). Throughout these editions, Harris is careful to point out and explain his own editorial decisions.

All great writers teach us how to read their texts but, as Harris asserts, "Burroughs is training us how to read the culture around us, or rather the culture *inside* us" (*Ticket* xx). Burroughs contributes to a battle over the production of reality by offering his readers methods to escape the control of language and global media. He wants to change our consciousness through techniques that thwart the conventional and habitual. It is impossible to read these texts in any conventional manner, with preprogrammed narrative expectations. Instead, a reader becomes sensitive to patterns, echoes and emotions, intersections and transitions in a carefully crafted, complex intertextual network of what Burroughs describes as "association lines." In a bravura feat of close reading, Harris demonstrates how images related to the fair (the St. Louis World's Fair of 1904, the song "Johnny's So Long at the Fair," fairground rides) throughout these three books and other works by Burroughs circulate and signal to adventurous readers about "the broken promises of desire" and "the enduring pain of personal loss—nostalgically for childhood innocence, melancholically for love—and its manipulation according to the false promises and addictive kicks of consumer capitalism" (*Ticket* xxi–xxiii).

Readings are enriched through Harris's source identification. A mysterious addition to the 1967 edition of the chapter "showed you your air" in *Ticket* originates from an art-historical source and refers to a then-recent act of Situationist sabotage, an attack in April 1964 by the Danish artist Jørgen Nash and other members of *Bauhaus Situationniste*, who decapitated the Little Mermaid statue in Copenhagen harbor (*Ticket* 280).

> The Old Man himself stood at the end of the board room table a hat box under his arm. With an abrupt movement he emptied the hat box. The bronze head of a young girl crudely severed with a hack saw clattered across the board room table. The Old Man held up a hack saw bronze filings caught in its teeth. "This old hand went and sawed the head off their filthy mermaid ... J. Ericson & Sisters only living rival of Trak If anyone does not like this thing that I have done I can use this saw a second time." (*Ticket* 197)

Harris's new edition of the Cut-Up Trilogy will be an invaluable and necessary resource for Burroughs scholars and anyone interested in experimental literature. My only reservation about this new edition concerns Harris's decision to drop the essay "the invisible generation" from *Ticket*. As in the 1962 edition, Bryon Gysin's calligraphy appears on the same page as the conclusion to *Ticket*, but Harris's edition also includes the final three lines Burroughs added to his 1967 edition: "See the action, B. J.? This Hassan I Sabbah really works for Naval Intelligence and .. Are you listening B.J.?" (230). Harris offers a powerful aesthetic argument for his decision to eliminate "the invisible generation": "The composite formed by print and script ends the most musical book of the Cut-Up Trilogy on a soundless note" (li-lii). He describes the essay as of "historical interest" (Ticket li), sends interested readers to *Word Virus: The William S. Burroughs Reader* (218-24), and refers to key passages from the essay in the Notes. However, I missed the visceral impact of confronting the unpunctuated essay after Gysin's calligraphy. I find the abrupt contrast between the elegiac ending of *Ticket* and the insistent, activist encouragement of the essay strangely compelling, a dynamic reminder that the literary is also a call to action for individuals. The essay, with its open-ended conclusion and Shakespearean echo, "cut the prerecordings into air into thin air," complements potential readings of the expanded role of tape recorders in the new narrative additions to *Ticket*, and responds to the cheeky conclusion, "Are you listening, B. J.?" Harris argues that "[g]iven the book's project to transcend time, it would be ironic to fetishize the past and deny change by repeating the products of particular historical circumstances" (*Ticket* li), but isn't this irony a potential hazard for any genetic reading? On the contrary, awareness of the complex open endings of both the Olympia and Grove editions of *Ticket* offer new possibilities for creative readings of Burroughs's relentless provocations that any number can play.

— Katharine Streip, *Concordia University*

Works Cited

Bolton, Michael Sean. *Mosaic of Juxtaposition: William S. Burroughs' Narrative Revolution*. Amsterdam, New York: Rodopi, 2014. Print.

Murphy, Timothy S. *Wising Up the Marks: The Amodern William Burroughs*. Berkeley: U of California P, 1997. Print.

The Beat Index 2013-16

"The Beat Index" provides a chronicle of recent scholarship, including dissertations, in the field of Beat Studies. The artists and other Beat Generation figures represented here are core to the movement or are associated with then-contemporary and complementary avant-garde poetic movements. Unless otherwise noted, abstracts featured in the "Index" are publisher/author abstracts, and some are excerpted for purposes of continuity. Texts are organized within categories from most to least recent and range alphabetically according to author. The entries recommence from volume 3 (2014) of the *Journal of Beat Studies* and extend through January 2016.

We intend the Index to be as comprehensive as possible. If we have omitted a title, the editors will greatly appreciate being informed of that omission so that we can include the title in the next volume of this journal.

Beats as a Group/Movement

2016

Carmona, Christopher, Rob Johnson, and Chuck Taylor. Eds. *The Beatest State in the Union: an Anthology of Beat Texas Writing*. Beaumont, TX: Lamar UP, 2016.

> Many of the major Beat writers of the 1950s and 1960s had a fascination with Texas. They spent time there, traveled around the state, wrote there. And left a legacy among the Texas writers they met as well as those influenced by reading the original Beats. This anthology includes both well known Beat writers and contemporary writers in the process of making names for themselves with their publications.

Morgan, Bill. *The Beats Abroad: A Global Guide to the Beat Generation*. San Francisco: City Lights, 2016.

> Morgan documents that international phase of the Beat Generation's story. He delves into epicenters like Paris, Tangier, and Mexico City, and tracks down more remote locales from Siberia to Colombia. Entries contain specific addresses for the globetrotting reader to visit on every continent and are loaded with fascinating stories that illuminate the lives and works of Ginsberg, Burroughs, Corso, Kerouac, Ferlinghetti, and others during

their travels abroad. This handy reference lets the reader trace Ginsberg's trail through India, or find the hotel in Tangier where Burroughs wrote *Naked Lunch*, and more.

2015

City Lights Pocket Poets Anthology. 60th Anniversary Edition. Ed. Lawrence Ferlinghetti. San Francisco: City Light, 2015.

> A landmark retrospective celebrating sixty years of publishing and cultural history, this edition provides an invaluable distillation of the energetic, iconoclastic, and still fresh body of work represented in the ongoing series. Ferlinghetti has selected poems from each of its sixty volumes, including the work of Ginsberg, Kerouac, Corso, Pasolini, Voznesensky, Prevert, Mayakovsky, Cortazar, O'Hara, Ponsot, Levertov, di Prima, Duncan, Lamantia, Lowry, and others.

Cottrell, Robert C. *Sex, Drugs, and Rock 'n' Roll: The Rise of America's 1960s Counterculture*. Lanham: Rowman & Littlefield, 2015.

> Cottrell examines American bohemia, the lyrical left of the pre-World War II era, the hipsters, and the Beats on the East and West coasts, as well as in the American heartland. He delivers something of a collective biography through an exploration of the antics of seminal countercultural figures Allen Ginsberg, Jack Kerouac, Timothy Leary, and Ken Kesey. Cottrell also presents fascinating chapters covering "the magic elixir of sex," rock 'n roll, the underground press, Haight-Ashbury, the literature that garnered the attention of many in the counterculture, Monterey Pop, the Summer of Love, "the Death of Hippie," the March on the Pentagon, communes, Yippies, Weatherman, Woodstock, the Manson family, the women's movement, and the decade's legacies.

Reid, Michael. *The Beats in Denver. A Self-Guided Tour: Where Kerouac, Cassady and Ginsberg Hung Out*. N.p.: High Street Press, 2015.

> Containing passages from works by Jack Kerouac, Neal Cassady, and Allen Ginsberg describing where they hung out in Denver, this is a comprehensive guide to an important Beat Generation city. It includes a number of specific tours with many sites featured for the first time. Readers can follow the step-by-step directions or plug the addresses into a phone or GPS.

Weldman, Rich. *The Beat Generation FAQ: All That's Left to Know About the Angelheaded Hipsters*. Milwaukee: Beatback, 2015.

> The Beat Generation FAQ is an informative and entertaining look at the enigmatic authors and cutting-edge works that shaped this fascinating cultural and literary movement. Beat Generation writers were no strangers to controversy: Both Allen Ginsberg's prophetic, William Blakean-style poem "Howl" (1956) and William S. Burroughs's groundbreaking novel *Naked Lunch* (1959) led to obscenity trials, while Jack Kerouac's highly influential novel *On the Road* (1957) was blamed by the establishment for corrupting the nation's youth and continues to this day to serve as a beacon of hipster culture and the bohemian lifestyle. Although the movement as a whole flamed out quickly in the early 1960s, replaced by the onset of the hippie counterculture, the Beats made an indelible mark on the nation's consciousness and left a long-lasting influence on its art and culture. This book details the movement. including its works, creative forces, and legacy.

Yulianto, Henrikus Joko. "Beatnik Spontaneity in the American Beat Poetry as the Image of Culture Rebels: Fostering and Transmitting a Vision of Socio-Ecological Wisdoms." *The Image of the Rebel*. Pueblo: Colorado State UP, 2015. 54-64.

2014

Tytell, John. *Writing Beat and Other Occasions of Literary Mayhem*. Nashville: Vanderbilt UP, 2014. 54-64.

> A preeminent historian of Beat culture, Tytell positions himself as an eyewitness to the literary movement of Jack Kerouac, Allen Ginsberg, William S. Burroughs, and others. As he interviewed, drank, traveled, and survived countless moments with some of these literary legends, Tytell discovered much about the craft of nonfiction and biography, and the nature of history. *Writing Beat* demonstrates, through Tytell's growth as a professor and historian of the Beats, lessons learned and hazards encountered for those aspiring to become writers themselves.

Versluis, Arthus. *American Gurus: From Transcendentalism to New Age Religion*. New York: Oxford UP, 2014.

By the early twenty-first century, a phenomenon that once was inconceivable had become nearly commonplace in American society: the public spiritual teacher who neither belongs to, nor is authorized by, a major religious tradition. *American Gurus* tells the story of how this phenomenon emerged. Through an examination of the broader literary and religious context of the subject, Versluis shows that a characteristic feature of the Western esoteric tradition is the claim that every person can achieve "spontaneous, direct, unmediated spiritual insight." This claim was articulated with special clarity by the New England Transcendentalists Bronson Alcott and Ralph Waldo Emerson. Versluis explores Transcendentalism, Walt Whitman, the Beat movement, Timothy Leary, and the New Age movement to shed light on the emergence of the contemporary American guru.

Woznicki, John, Ed. *The New American Poetry: Fifty Years Later.* Bethlehem, PA: Lehigh UP, 2014.

This book is a collection of critical essays on Donald Allen's 1960 seminal anthology, *The New American Poetry*, which Marjorie Perloff once called "the fountain head of radical American poetics." Allen's anthology has reached its 50th anniversary, providing a unique time for reflection and reevaluation of this preeminent collection. The volume goes beyond the analysis of construction and reception and achieves something distinctive, extending those former treatments by treading on the paths they create in order to discover another sense of "radical"—as in the sense of root, of harboring something fundamental, something inherent.

2013

Carmona, Christopher Richard. "Keeping The Beat: The Practice of a Beat Movement." *Dissertation Abstracts International* 74.3 (2013).

From the popularization of hitchhiking across America to the rebel without a cause of James Dean, the Hippie movement of the '60s, and the explosion of poetry readings in coffee shops, the Beats have been influential to much of the social change in the last half-century. Commonly the architects of the movement are referenced as Jack Kerouac, Allen Ginsberg, and William S. Burroughs. However, the Beat Generation was much bigger than three white men who wrote novels and poetry about disenfranchised youths of the 1950s.

Pawlik, Joanna. "Surrealism, Beat Literature, and the San Francisco Renaissance." *Literature Compass* 10.2 (2013): 97-110.

> This article explores the reception of Surrealism in postwar American poetry, focusing on Beat and San Francisco Renaissance writers' responses to the movement. Existing scholarship on Surrealism's presence in twentieth-century American poetry has tended to differentiate between the small number of writers who joined Breton's circle, and the large number of poets whose work testifies to the movement's protean yet extensive influence on modern and postmodern verse. Taking Beat and San Francisco Renaissance writers as a case study, this article seeks to interrogate such classifications, arguing that a writer's "distance" from the epicenter of the movement is not necessarily a reliable guide to the nature of their interactions with Surrealism. For instance, though not a member of the group per se, Allen Ginsberg had extensive contact with the movement and he and his Beat colleagues helped redefine Surrealism's postwar currency and profile. Ahistorical assertions of basic similarities or differences between Beat writers and narrow definitions of Surrealism cannot capture the dynamics and complexities of these dialogues.

Petrich, Tatum L. "The Girl Gang: Women Writers of the New York City Beat Community." *Dissertation Abstracts International* 73.10 (2013).

> This dissertation engages the lives and work of five women Beat writers (Diane di Prima, Joyce Johnson, Hettie Jones, Carol Bergé, and Mimi Albert) to argue that, from a position of marginality, these women developed as protofeminist writers, interrogating the traditional female gender role and constructing radical critiques of normative ideas in fiction and poetry in ways that resisted the male Beats' general subordination of women and that anticipated the feminist movement of the late 1960s and 1970s. A project of recovery and criticism, "The Girl Gang" provides literary biographies that explore how each writer's experience as a marginalized female writer within an otherwise countercultural community affected the development of her work; it also analyzes a range of works (published and unpublished texts from various genres, written from the early 1950s through the turn of the twenty-first century) in order to illustrate how each writer distinctively employs and revises mainstream and Beat literary and cultural conventions, including fundamental Beat questions of identity, authenticity, and subjectivity.

Vogel, Andrew. "The Dream and the Dystopia: Bathetic Humor, the Beats, and Walt Whitman's Idealism." *Amerikastudien/American Studies* 58.3 (2013): 389-407.

> Among the many influences on the Beats, none looms larger than Walt Whitman from whom they adopted a vision of democratic equality, potent artistic honesty, and forthright sexual expression. The distance between Whitman's vision of American and the dystopia described in "Howl" animated the Beats' literary project, but it also propagated an abiding sense of ideological doubt. This is one of the primary bases of the Beat ethos. When Beat writers invoke the distance between Whitman's idealistic dream of democratic vistas and the dystopia of 1950s America, they frequently do so in ways that are comical or that depict characters laughing. The distance between Whitman's dream and the Beats' dystopia is hardly a laughing matter, however, making such humor bathetic. Bathos can be defined as the laughable result of straining for a sublime ideal but tripping over hard reality into the absurd. Despite their range of forms and styles, Allen Ginsberg, John Clellon Holmes, Jack Kerouac, and Gary Snyder all reflect the bathetic impulse.

Jack Kerouac

2015

Barnstone, Willis. "On the Road from Dante to Jack Kerouac (Stopping by Frost, Pound, and Eliot)." *Comparative Literature Studies*. 52. 2 (2015).

> Dante is a unique epic poet whose medium is song, the canto. He is also a cruel theologian punishing not only lovers for misbehavior, but also the great pre-Christian figures like his guide Virgil for not having been baptized. Through love, he journeys to the highest Empyrean where, guided by evermore beautiful and remote Beatrice, he is enveloped in light and can see God. On the other hand, Kerouac's ecstatic love takes place not with angels of the *Primum Mobile* but with wild outsiders like himself. He seeks his way through the Inferno to find Zen satori. In this essay, Barnstone illuminates parallels between Dante's cantos and Sal Paradise's epic-like adventures.

Gipko, Jesse. "Road Narratives as Cultural Critiques: Henry Miller, Jack Kerouac, John Steinbeck, and William Least Heat-Moon." *Dissertation Abstracts International* 76.4 (2015).

> Since the advent of the automobile in the early twentieth century, Americans have been preoccupied with traveling the continent in ways that resonate with the country's history of exploration and expansion. The American road narrative began as an exploration of the beauty and diversity of the country and as a way to explore self, but it soon emerged as a vehicle for writers to examine the country and comment on change and progress—but not always positively. As America transformed throughout the twentieth century, the hope of individuality and self-expression articulated by Ralph Waldo Emerson, Henry David Thoreau, and Walt Whitman morphed into a critique of the growing conformity, homogenization, and consumer culture that was equally feared by these writers. Hope for the ideals inherent in America coupled with a disappointment when they fail to become manifest in the country are an integral part of the road narratives in this study: Henry Miller's *The Air-Conditioned Nightmare,* Jack Kerouac's *On the Road,* John Steinbeck's *Travels with Charley,* and William Least Heat-Moon's *Blue Highways*. These road narratives engage with and critique conditions in the post-Great Depression.

Kupetz, Joshua. "'Spastic Saints': Jack Kerouac, Non-Conformity, and Disability Representation." *Journal of Literary & Cultural Disability Studies.* 9.2 (2015).

> Jack Kerouac uses representations of disability throughout his fictional narratives to signify radical social non-conformity. Such representations are often considered acts of "discursive subjugation," in the words of David T. Mitchell and Sharon L. Snyder, but the affinity between symbolic representation and the political as such can open a space for a figural use of disability that does not marginalize. Kerouac's *The Town and the City* (1950) offers two disabled characters, Waldo Meister and Jimmy Bannon, who not only embody metaphors but also demonstrate productive, often contradictory effects of disability representation. Both Meister and Bannon flip the script of disability representation by signifying an emergent common U.S. subjectivity triangulated with the ideological modernity of the backward-looking small town and the proto-postmodernity of the forward-looking metropolis. In *On the Road* (1957), Kerouac extends his use of disability as a marker of non-conformist opposition to the dehumanizing hegemony of late capitalism. Dean Moriarty's disability

provides him with an alternative subject position that frees him frompostwar hypermasculinity, and Kerouac uses phalangeal amputation as a textual motif that signifies social non-conformist affiliation, not social stigmatization.

Wilcke, Jonathon. "'With No Outcome In Mind': Improvisation and Improvisational Poetics in 20th-Century North American Poetry." *Dissertation Abstracts International* 75.7 (2015).

Using an interdisciplinary methodology drawn from musicology, poetics, cultural theory, and the branch of musical improvisation known as "free improvisation," this dissertation defines and categorizes improvisation and improvisational practices in twentieth-century North American poetry and poetics. Beginning with the contention that improvisation is an under-articulated concept in the field of contemporary poetics, the dissertation proceeds to categorically define the most iconic and successful improvisational strategies in North American poetry. Under the rubric of "idiomatic poetic improvisation," Wilcke examines the improvisational strategies in the work of Jack Kerouac, Kenneth Rexroth, Kenneth Patchen, Amiri Baraka, and Nathaniel Mackey. Under "non-idiomatic improvisation," Wilcke discusses the following writers: David Antin, Lyn Hejinian, Steve Benson, William Carlos Williams, and Andrew Levy. Steve McCaffery, Jackson Mac Low, and the Four Horsemen's approach to performed poetic improvisation also fall under this second category.

2014

Bristow, Daniel "New Spellings: Auto-Orthographies in *Zami and Vanity of Duluoz*." *Life Writing*. 11. 3 (2014): 275-292.

Cantani, Damian Paul. "Re/Deconstructing the Rimbaud Myth: Kerouac and Mallarmé." *AmeriQuests*, 11.1 (2014).

Garcia-Robles, Jorge. *At the End of the Road: Jack Kerouac in Mexico*. Trans. Daniel C. Schechter. Minneapolis, MN: U of Minnesota P, 2014.

Mexico, an escape route, inspiration, and ecstatic terminus of the celebrated novel *On the Road*, was crucial to Jack Kerouac's creative development. In this dramatic and highly compelling account, García-Robles, leading authority on the Beats in Mexico, recreates both the actual events and the literary imaginings of Kerouac in what became the writer's revelatory terrain. Providing Kerouac an immediate spiritual freshness that contrasted with the staid society of the United States, Mexico was perhaps the single most important country in his life. Sourcing material from the Beat author's vast output and revealing correspondence, García-Robles vividly describes the milieu and people that influenced him while sojourning there and the circumstances between his myriad arrivals and departures. From the writer's initial euphoria upon encountering Mexico and its fascinating tableau of humanity to his tortured relationship with a Mexican prostitute who inspired his novella *Tristessa*, this volume chronicles Kerouac's often illusory view of the country while realistically detailing the incidents and individuals that found their way into his poetry and prose.

Iadonisi, Richard A. "The Masculine Urge of Jack Kerouac's Haiku," *The Journal of American Culture*. 37. 3 (2014): 290-298.

During the 1950s, Beat writers dissatisfied with the state of both American culture and literature sought a cure for Western ills in Japanese philosophy (Zen Buddhism in particular) and poetry (haiku in particular). Among the prominent Beats to produce haiku are Gary Snyder, Allen Ginsberg, Philip Whalen, and Cid Corman. However, perhaps the most interesting Beat haiku writer is Jack Kerouac, far better known for his sprawling novels. Although the 2003 publication of *Book of Haikus* sparked a renewed interest in the 500-plus haiku that Kerouac wrote, critics initially dismissed these three-line poems.

Keilty, Rebecca. "Kerouac in Florida." *Journal of Florida Studies*. 1.3 (2014)

An extremely brief overview of Kerouac's life and death in Florida.

Kerouac, Jack. *The Haunted Life: and Other Writings*. Ed. Todd Tietchen. Boston: Da Capo, 2014.

At some point in 1944, under circumstances that remain rather mysterious, Kerouac lost a novella-length manuscript entitled *The Haunted Life*. A coming-of-age story about Peter Martin, this fictional treatment of his hometown of Lowell, Massachusetts, is set against the backdrop of the everyday: the comings and goings of the shopping district, the banter and braggadocio that occurs within the smoky atmospherics of the corner bar, the drowsy sound of a baseball game over the radio. Peter is heading into his sophomore year at Boston College, and while home for the summer, he struggles with the pressing issues of his day: the economic crisis of the previous decade and what appears to be the impending entrance of the United States into the Second World War. The other principal characters, Garabed Tourian and Dick Sheffield, are based respectively on Sebastian Sampas and fellow Lowellian Billy Chandler, both of whom had already died in combat by the time of Kerouac's drafting of *The Haunted Life* (providing some of the impetus for its title). Garabed is a leftist idealist and poet, with a pronounced tinge of the Byronic. Dick is a romantic adventurer whose wanderlust has him poised to leave Galloway for the wider world, with or without Peter. *The Haunted Life* also contains a compelling and controversial portrayal of Jack's father, Leo Kerouac, recast as Joe Martin.

2013

Lane, Veronique. "The Parting of Burroughs and Kerouac: The French Backstory to the First Beat Novel, from Rimbaud to Poetic Realist Cinema." *Comparative American Studies: An International Journal.* 11. 3 (2013): 265-279.

> JBS Abstract: Lane analyzes *And The Hippos Were Boiled in Their Tanks*, co-written by Jack Kerouac and William S. Burroughs, focusing specifically on Kerouac's "I Wish I Were You," arguing that he used this little-known text to distance himself as a writer from Burroughs and to initiate his experiments with the bookmovie. Lane claims that this early text illustrates the importance of French avant-garde literature and philosophy in the development of Kerouac's Beat aesthetics, more so than his own Quebecois culture.

Ording, Dominic. "Paradoxes Along the Beat Journey in Kerouac's *On The Road.*" *American Road Literature.* Ipswich, MA: Salem, 2013. 81-100.

William S. Burroughs

2015

Winslow, Aaron W. "The Labor of the Avant-Garde: Experimental Form and the Politics of Work in Post-War American Poetry and Fiction." *Dissertation Abstracts International* 76.6 (2015).

While literary critics have explored the politics of labor in pre-war modernist literature, the post-1945 avant-garde has continued to be framed as a depoliticized repetition of previous avant-garde styles. Examining American avant-garde literature in its relation to the political and economic shifts from the 1960s through the late 1980s, this dissertation corrects this narrative to show that labor and labor politics were central categories in post-war experimental poetry and fiction. Winslow argues that writers as disparate as Charles Olson, William S. Burroughs, Samuel R. Delany, and Susan Howe reworked disjunctive modernist forms to cognitively map emergent economic tendencies in the United States.

2014

Bolton, Michael Sean. *Mosaic of Juxtaposition: William S. Burroughs' Narrative Revolution*. Amsterdam: Rodopi P, 2014.

> William S. Burroughs's experimental narratives, from the 1959 publication of *Naked Lunch* through the late trilogy of the 1980s, have provided readers with intriguing challenges and, for some, disheartening frustrations. Yet these novels continue to generate new interest and inspire new insights among an increasing and evolving readership. This book addresses the unique characteristics of Burroughs's narrative style in order to discover strategies for engaging and navigating these demanding novels. Burroughs's subversive themes and randomizing techniques do not amount to unmitigated attacks on conventions, as many critics suggest, but constitute part of a careful strategy for effecting transformations in his readers. Utilizing various poststructuralist theories, as well as recent theories in electronic literature and posthumanism, *Mosaic of Juxtaposition* examines the various strategies that Burroughs employs to challenge assumptions about textual interpretation and to redefine the relationship between reader and text.

Burroughs, William S. *Taking Shots: The Photography of William S. Burroughs*. Ed. Patricia Allmer and John Sears. Munich: Prestel, 2014.

> Marking the centenary of William S. Burroughs's birth, this book reproduces the celebrated writer's many rarely seen photographs. Renowned and highly regarded for his experiments with literature, painting, film, and music, Burroughs was also a prolific photographer. However, his photographic work, consisting of several thousand images, has so far

received little critical attention or sustained public exposure. This book provides convincing evidence that his photographs should be considered a significant aspect of his entire body of work. It includes portraits and self-portraits, location images from his travels in Europe, the Americas, and North Africa, images of construction and demolition sites, and his individual and collaborative experiments with photomontage, assemblage, and collage. Essays by internationally acclaimed scholars of photography and of Burroughs's work offer a variety of critical perspectives on his photographic oeuvre, examining its sources, methodologies, biographical contexts, influences, and purposes. Contributors include Barry Miles, Susan Laxton, and David Brittain.

Harrison, K. C. "Lerio Jones's Radio and the Literary 'Break' from Ellison to Burroughs." *African American Review* 47.2-3 (2014): 357-374.
See entry under LeRoi Jones.

Miles, Barry. *William S. Burroughs.* London: Weidenfeld & Nicolson, 2014.
See review in this volume of the *Journal of Beat Studies.*

Shoaf, Eric C. *William S. Burroughs: A Collector's Guide*. Inkblot, 2014.

The purpose of this volume is to provide a gathering of Burroughs material published through 2008, which includes well over a thousand different items: books, pamphlets, limited editions, signed editions, magazine or journal contributions, contributions to the works of other authors, or simply books and other printed biographical material about Burroughs.

2013

Davis, Stephen. *William Burroughs / Local Stop on the Nova Express*. Providence: RI: Inkblot, 2013.

This volume features the long-lost interview with author William S. Burroughs, never reprinted since its first appearance in *The Real Paper* in 1974. The Introduction treats Burroughs's life and work, while Part 3 is an overview of the discussion between Burroughs and Jimmy Page printed in *Crawdaddy* in 1975. Author/interviewer is noted rock biographer and journalist Stephen Davis, known for his books on Led Zeppelin, Jim Morrison, The Rolling Stones, Bob Marley, Aerosmith, and others.

Lane, Veronique. "The Parting of Burroughs and Kerouac: The French Backstory to the First Beat Novel, From Rimbaud to Poetic Realist Cinema." *Comparative American Studies: An International Journal* 11.3 (2013): 265-279. See entry under Kerouac.

MacFayden, Ian. *William S. Burroughs: Cut (The Future of the Past)*. Köln, Germany: Walther König, 2013.

> As William S. Burroughs developed from an author of novels and short stories into a "cosmonaut of inner space" and a technician of consciousness, he expanded his experiments beyond the confines of fiction, pursuing the implications of his cut-up technique into film, painting, collage, and audio experiments. Many of these investigations, which gained momentum during Burroughs's Paris and London years in the 1960s, were done as collaborations. Burroughs believed that creative collaboration produced something he called "The Third Mind"—a creative entity or will distinct from that of any single participant, which nonetheless could not exist without them. By the mid-1960s, he was treating the method as an occult operation, after prophesying various deaths and disasters by cut-up and collaboration. This volume looks at the collages, scrapbooks, films, and audio works made by Burroughs in collaboration with his mentor Brion Gysin (with whom he authored the book *The Third Mind*), London filmmaker Anthony Balch, and electronics technician Ian Sommerville, as well as his later collaborations with writers and artists such as John Giorno and George Condo. An interview with Burroughs conducted by Jean-Jacques Lebel in Paris in 1982 is included, published here for the first time in English.

Allen Ginsberg

2016

Ginsberg, Allen. *Wait Till I'm Dead: Uncollected Poems* Ed. Bill Morgan. New York: Grove Press, 2016.

> The first new Ginsberg collection in over 15 years, *Wait Till I'm Dead* is a landmark publication, edited by renowned Ginsberg scholar Bill Morgan and introduced by award-winning poet and Ginsberg enthusiast Rachel Zucker. Ginsberg wrote incessantly for more than 50 years, often composing poetry on demand, and many of the poems collected in

this volume were scribbled in letters or sent off to obscure publications and unjustly forgotten. *Wait Till I'm Dead,* which spans the whole of Ginsberg's long writing career from the 1940s to the 1990s, is a testament to Ginsberg's astonishing writing and singular aesthetics. Following the chronology of his life, *Wait Till I'm Dead* reproduces the poems together with extensive notes. Containing 104 previously uncollected poems and accompanied by original photographs, *Wait Till I'm Dead* is the final major contribution to Ginsberg's oeuvre.

2015

Katz, Eliot. *The Poetry and Politics of Allen Ginsberg.* St. Andrews, U.K.: Beatdom Books, 2015.

Allen Ginsberg was one of the most politically engaged writers of his era, with a widespread social and cultural impact that was rare for a poet of his or any generation. In this volume, Katz takes a readable, scholarly look at Ginsberg's most influential poems and explores the varied and inventive ways that Ginsberg turned his political ideas and perceptions into powerful poetry. While there have been some important previous biographies and other books looking at Ginsberg's life and work, this is the first full-length volume focusing primarily on how Ginsberg's writing works as political poetry and on Ginsberg's extraordinary influence on political culture over the ensuing decades. As a longtime poet and activist himself, as well as a friend of Ginsberg's who worked with him on a number of poetry and activist endeavors, Katz brings a unique personal, political, and literary perspective to this project. This book—including its chapter on "Howl," which offers an astute and original guide to reading Ginsberg's most celebrated poem—will be of interest to students and scholars studying Ginsberg's poetry in college classrooms, as well as to general readers and writers who enjoy Ginsberg's work.

Morgan, Bill, Ed. *I Greet You at the Beginning of a Great Career: The Selected Correspondence of Lawrence Ferlinghetti and Allen Ginsberg, 1955-1997.* San Francisco: City Lights, 2015.

In 1969, Allen Ginsberg wrote to his friend, fellow poet, and publisher Lawrence Ferlinghetti, "Alas, telephone destroys letters!" Fortunately, however, by then the two had already exchanged a treasure trove of personal correspondence, and more than any other documents, their letters—intimate, opinionated, and action-packed—reveal the true nature of their lifelong friendship and creative relationship. Collected here for the first time, they offer an intimate view into the range of artistic vision and complementary sensibilities that fueled the genius of their literary collaborations. The majority of the letters collected here have never before been published, and they span the period from 1955 until Ginsberg's death in 1997. Facsimiles and photographs enhance the collection, an evocative portrait of an inspiring and enduring relationship.

2013

Ferris, William R. "Trading Verses: James 'Son Ford' Thomas and Allen Ginsberg." *Southern Cultures* 19. 1 (2013): 53-60.

Kearful, Frank J. "Alimentary Poetics: Robert Lowell and Allen Ginsberg."*Partial Answers: Journal of Literature and the History of Ideas* 11. 1 (2013): 87-108.

> Robert Lowell coined the famous distinction between cooked and raw poetry, but beginning with Joel Barlow's epic treat, *The Hasty Pudding*, there is a long tradition of American poetics sustained by copious and artful use of tropes of hunger, food, and eating. Allen Ginsberg's *Howl and Other Poems* and Lowell's *Life Studies* would be emaciated beyond recognition without them. Also taking other poems into account, the essay argues that Lowell and Ginsberg did more to enrich the American alimentary poetic tradition than anyone else since T. S. Eliot and Wallace Stevens.

Prabhu, Gayathri. "Figurations of the Spiritual Squalid in Allen Ginsberg's *Indian Journals*: Transformation of India in Post-War Beat and American Imagination" *Transnational Literature* 6. 1 (2013).

> This article explores the impact that India had on Beat imagination with specific emphasis on Ginsberg's under-studied Indian Journals, written during his travels in India in 1962-63, and published in 1970. The earlier American literary view of India was dominated by the notion of the spiritual East and was evoked in the high prose of Emerson and Whitman. In the new context and historical time of post-war counterculture, India came to constitute a different kind of repertoire: 1) the trope of physical travel (unlike the earlier literary forebears who had never actually visited India) and its sense of encounter with the untranscendable physical "dirt" of India, 2) India as a new realm of the sexual (in contrast with

the more traditional dominant trend of India as "ascetic spiritual") and the intertwining of the sexual and spiritual, and 3) experimentation with drugs to explore the spaces between pilgrimage and tourism wherein India as a whole and in itself offers alternate states of bodily being. Moving away from conventional postcolonial notions of "representation" in modes that might still be seen as quasi-Orientalist, Prabhu reads Ginsberg's text as creating a new kind of literary and aesthetic density, mixing genres of travelogue, diary, poetry, confession, doodle, and photography. In contrast to the entirely uni-directional notions of Orientalist representation, Prabhu argues that this encounter re-defined Beat notions of space, sexuality, and alternate consciousness.

Swope, Richard. "Allen Ginsberg and the Beats in Literary Paris, or Apollinaire through the Door of Ginsberg's Mind." *American Writers in Europe: 1850 to the Present*. New York: Palgrave Macmillan, 2013. 187-206.

JBS Abstract: This essay attempts to fill in a gap in Ginsberg scholarship by offering a close reading of the poem "At Apollinaire's Grave." Ginsberg's poem celebrates Apollinaire's contributions as well as the profound influence he and the larger Paris avant-garde had on Ginsberg himself.

Amiri Baraka (LeRoi Jones)

2015

Baraka, Amiri. *S O S: Poems* 1961-2013. Ed. Paul Vangelisti. New York: Grove, 2015.

Fusing the personal and the political in high-voltage verse, Amiri Baraka was one of the preeminent literary innovators of the past century. Selected by Paul Vangelisti, this volume comprises the fullest spectrum of Baraka's rousing revolutionary poems, from his first collection to previously unpublished pieces composed during his final years. Throughout Baraka's career as a prolific writer (also published as LeRoi Jones), he was vehemently outspoken against oppression of African American citizens, and he radically altered the discourse surrounding racial inequality. The environments and social values that inspired his poetics changed during the course of his life, a trajectory that can be traced in this retrospective spanning more than five decades of profoundly evolving subjects and techniques. Praised for its lyricism and introspection, his early poetry emerged from the Beat Generation, while his later writing is marked by intensely rebellious fervor and subversive ideology. All along, his primary focus was on how to live and love in the present moment despite the enduring difficulties of human history.

GwinnLandry, Mark M. "Epistemology Of The Veil." *Dissertation Abstracts International* 75.8 (2015).

Drawing upon a set of cultural artifacts that span almost a century—from Frederick Douglass's publication of *Life and Times of Frederick Douglass* (1892) to dispatches from the frontlines of the race war staged in Amiri Baraka's *The Slave* (1964)—this dissertation examines a protracted history of American artists' reinscribing Shakespeare's *Othello* to sound the deep structure of American culture and confront the pathology of its white privilege. Throughout his peculiar American career attending to the racial crises dividing America's body politic, the Moor of Venice has remained a totemic figure of American cultural totality as it is supersaturated by racial animus.

Maxwell, William J. *F. B. Eyes: How J. Edgar Hoover's Ghostreaders Framed African American Literature*. Princeton: Princeton UP, 2015.

Few institutions seem more opposed than African American literature and J. Edgar Hoover's Federal Bureau of Investigation. But behind the scenes, the FBI's hostility to black protest was energized by fear of and respect for black writing. Drawing on nearly 14,000 pages of newly released FBI files, *F.B. Eyes* exposes the Bureau's intimate policing of five decades of African American poems, plays, essays, and novels. Starting in 1919, year one of Harlem's renaissance and Hoover's career at the Bureau, secretive FBI "ghostreaders" monitored the latest developments in African American letters. By the time of Hoover's death in 1972, these ghostreaders knew enough to simulate a sinister black literature of their own. The official aim behind the Bureau's close reading was to anticipate political unrest. Yet, as William J. Maxwell reveals, FBI surveillance came to influence the creation and public reception of African American literature in the heart of the twentieth century.

Simanga, Michael. *Amiri Baraka and the Congress of African People: History And Memory*. New York: Palgrave Macmillan, 2015.

This discussion of the Congress of African People (CAP) combines historical research and analysis with the author's first-hand experience with the organization, providing the first historical narrative of a consequential player in the Black Power Movement.

Wilcke, Jonathon. "'With No Outcome In Mind': Improvisation and Improvisational Poetics In 20th-Century North American Poetry." *Dissertation Abstracts International* 75.7 (2015).
See entry under Jack Kerouac.

2014

Azouz, Samy. "Black Theatre And Propaganda: Amiri Baraka's Adherence to the Negro Problem and Defense of the Question of Labor." *Americana: E-Journal Of American Studies In Hungary* 10.2 (2014).

Benston, Kimberly W. "Preface To A Twenty Volume Critical Note: For Amiri, Ghost Of The Future." *Callaloo* 37.3 (2014): 480-482.

Crawford, Margo Natalie. "Baraka's Jam Session: On The Limits Of Any Attempt To Collect Black Aesthetics Unbound." *Callaloo* 37.3 (2014): 477-479.

Goldsworthy, Joan, Christine Miner, and Deborah A. Ring. "Baraka, Amiri 1934-2014." *Contemporary Black Biography, Volume 118.* Farmington Hills, MI: Gale, 2014. 9-15.

Harris, William J. "Amiri Baraka's Adventures With The Out & The Gone." *Callaloo* 37.3 (2014): 483-485.

Harrison, K. C. "Leroi Jones's Radio And The Literary 'Break' From Ellison To Burroughs." *African American Review* 47.2-3 (2014): 357-374.

> *JBS* Abstract: Harrison argues that the technology of radio influenced Baraka's early style and provided a model for conflicting voices in *Preface to a Twenty-Volume Suicide Note* and *The System of Dante's Hell*. He links Baraka with William S. Burroughs, tracing a lineage to Ralph Ellison's use of the break.

Hyland, John. "'HOW YOU SOUND??': The Poet's Voice, Aura, and the Challenge of Listening to Poetry." *Sounding Out!: The Sound Studies Blog* (2014).

"In Memoriam: Amiri Baraka: October 7, 1934-January 9, 2014 [Special Section]." *Callaloo* 37.3 (2014): 471-489.

Nielson, Erik. "White Surveillance of the Black Arts." *African American Review* 47.1 (2014): 161-177.

Ross, Marlon Bryan. "Baraka's Truth." *Callaloo* 37.3 (2014): 472-476.

—. "An Interview With Ntozake Shange." *Callaloo* 37.3 (2014): 486-489.

RudeWalker, Sarah. "Knowledge Of The Face: The Mythic Hero in Dialogic Readings of Jay Wright and Amiri Baraka." *Callaloo* 37.2 (2014): 358-368.

Winks, Christopher. "Amiri Baraka: Phenomenologist of Jazz Spirit." *Black Music, Black Poetry: Blues and Jazz's Impact on African American Versification*. Farnham, U.K.: Ashgate, 2014. 99-109.

2013

Bennett, Michael Y. "Dominance and the Triumph of the White Trickster Over the Black Picaro in Amiri Baraka's *Great Goodness of Life: A Coon Show.*" *Callaloo* 36.2 (2013): 312-321.

Lierow, Lars. "The 'Black Man's Vision of the World': Rediscovering Black Arts Filmmaking and the Struggle for a Black Cinematic Aesthetic." *Black Camera: An International Film Journal* 4.2 (2013): 3-21.

> This essay recovers filmmaking efforts within the Black Arts Movement of the late 1960s and early 70s, namely the films created by Larry Neal, one of the movement's key theorists, in collaboration with artists such as Amiri Baraka, Edward Spriggs, and James Hinton, discovered in the Harvard Film Archive. It focuses on three finished films and one film that was never finished: the documentary films *Moving On Up* and *The New Ark*, a fictional story set in Harlem called *Holy Days*, and *Revolution in Black America*, which was an early documentary film project that, according to the archival record, was never completed. These films have so far not received any critical attention. Analyzing these film texts and the circumstances of their production, this essay attempts to write the Black Arts Movement into the history of black cinema and reopen the question of a black cinematic aesthetic, connecting the concept to the

black freedom struggle that simultaneously generated the early black film criticism to which scholarship of black film remains indebted. Bridging the movement and film history, in turn, also allows a rethinking of the Black Arts Movement and its involvement with mass popular culture.

Mathes, Carter. "The Sounds of Anti-Anti-Essentialism: Listening to Black Consciousness in the Classroom." *Sounding Out!: The Sound Studies Blog*. Web. 29 Jan. 2013.

Paek, Hwankie. "A Revolution as a Fable: A Case of Baraka's *The Slave*." *Journal of Modern British and American Drama* 26.3 (2013): 89-111.

Pisano, Claudia Moreno. *Amiri Baraka and Edward Dorn: The Collected Letters*. Albuquerque: U of New Mexico P, 2013.

> From the end of the 1950s through the middle of the 1960s, Amiri Baraka (1934-2014) and Edward Dorn (1929-1999), two self-consciously avant-garde poets, fostered an intense friendship primarily through correspondence. The early 1960s found both poets just beginning to publish and becoming public figures. Bonding around their commitment to new and radical forms of poetry and culture, Dorn and Baraka created an interracial friendship at precisely the moment when the Civil Rights Movement was becoming a powerful force in national politics. The major premise of the Dorn-Jones friendship as developed through their letters was artistic, but the range of subjects in the correspondence shows an incredible intersection between the personal and the public, providing a schematic map of what was vital in postwar American culture to those living through it. Their letters offer a vivid picture of American lives connecting around poetry during a tumultuous time of change and immense creativity. Reading through these correspondences allows access into personal biographies, and through these biographies, profound moments in American cultural history open themselves in a way not easily found in official channels of historical narrative and memory.

Pittman, Elizabeth. "Voicing The 'Law Of The Sea': Commemoration and Cultural Nationalism in August Wilson's *Gem of the Ocean*." *Culture, Theory, And Critique* 54.1 (2013): 19-36.

> In Wilson's play *Gem of the Ocean*, a young man, Citizen Barlow, is in search of personal redemption for causing another man's death. Citizen

seeks the aid of Aunt Ester who leads him on this perilous journey and in doing so reveals a communal ethos. In order to achieve absolution for his crime against the community, he must journey to the "City of Bones" at the bottom of the Atlantic: an imaginative voyage along a reverse Middle Passage. This essay situates *Gem of the Ocean* in an artistic relationship of influence with Amiri Baraka's revolutionary play *Slave Ship* and Black Arts era representations of the Middle Passage as well as the slave ship in codifying national collectivity. Wilson relegates the slave ship to metaphorical terrain, but Pittman suggests that Wilson's symbolic uses of water, more specifically the sea, function as epistemological vehicles that translate historical experiences through individual acts of conscious and empathic reconnection with unknowable experiences in the past. Situating this analysis in a growing body of work on Wilson's play, Pittman argues that *Gem of the Ocean* pushes against the intertwined concepts of history and memory and creates an ethic of theatrical witnessing.

Schultz, Kathy Lou. *The Afro-Modernist Epic And Literary History: Tolson, Hughes, Baraka*. New York: Palgrave Macmillan, 2013.

Analyzing the poets Melvin B. Tolson, Langston Hughes, and Amiri Baraka, this study charts the Afro-Modernist epic. Within the context of classical epic traditions, early twentieth-century American modernist long poems, and the griot traditions of West Africa, Schultz reveals diasporic consciousness in the representation of African American identities.

Willey, Ann. "A Bridge Over Troubled Waters: Jazz, Diaspora Discourse, and E. B. Dongala's 'Jazz And Palm Wine' as Response to Amiri Baraka's 'Answers In Progress.'" *Research in African Literatures* 44.3 (2013): 138-151.

This essay explores how Emmanuel Dongala's story "Jazz and Palm Wine" (1970) rewrites Amiri Baraka's story "Answers in Progress" (1967). Baraka's story calls for a black revolution based in futurist thinking and diaspora consciousness embodied in jazz. In rewriting Baraka, Dongala resists discourses of coherent and stable identity through a recasting of the aesthetic functions of futurism and jazz. Dongala's intertextual use of, and emendations to, Baraka's story suggests his discomfort with articulations of diaspora identity that, in the late 1960s, were increasingly defined by cultural symbols. In transposing Baraka's futurist fable of the revolution to the African continent, Dongala stresses that while aesthetic objects, even ones as universally appealing as jazz, can be equally affective in different contexts, those contexts generate dramatically different effects.

Williams, Darius Omar. "The Negro Ensemble Company: Beyond Black Fists from 1967 to 1978." *Dissertation Abstracts International* 74.2 (2013).

> This study identifies The Negro Ensemble Company's agenda through a close textual analysis of eight Negro Ensemble Company plays spanning 1967-1978. The analysis contrasts Amiri Baraka's blueprint for a militant separatist-based Black Nationalist Theatre to The Negro Ensemble Company's quest to move beyond the rhetoric of race. Each chapter is organized around specific investigative questions and theories that critically interact with the thematic resonances intoned in each play. Some of the questions considered are the following: How did The Negro Ensemble Company alter the representations of black performativity before and during the early 1960s? What is the link between The Black Arts Movement and The Negro Ensemble Company Movement? How did Black Nationalist theory help The Negro Ensemble Company to reframe black experience? How did the plays produced by The Negro Ensemble Company deconstruct historical black family traditions? How are the tensions of the transatlantic slave trade and primordial origins of the African Diaspora situated in some of these plays? How did The Negro Ensemble Company permanently alter the landscape of Black American Theatre? This dissertation examines The Negro Ensemble Company's deemphasizing of white oppression while probing its restaging of black subjectivity in relation to rather than in opposition to Western paternalism.

Zygmonski, Aimee. "Amiri Baraka and the Black Arts Movement." *The Cambridge Companion to African American Theatre*. Cambridge: Cambridge UP, 2013. 137-154.

Ann Charters

2015

Charters, Ann and Charles Olson. *Evidence of What Is Said: The Correspondence between Ann Charters and Charles Olson about History and Herman Melville*. Portland: Tavern Books, 2015.
See entry under Charles Olson.

Lawrence Ferlinghetti

2015

Ferlinghetti, Lawrence. *Writing Across the Landscape: Travel Journals 1960-2013*. Eds. Giada Diano and Matthew Gleeson. New York: Liveright, 2015.

> Embedded with facsimile manuscript pages and an array of poems, many never before published, *Writing Across the Landscape* traverses the latter half of the twentieth century. For those only familiar with his poetry, these pages present a Ferlinghetti never before encountered, an elegant prose stylist and tireless political activist who was warning against the pernicious sins of our ever-expansive corporate culture long before such thoughts seeped into mainstream consciousness. Evoking each journey with a mixture of travelogue and poetry as well as his own hand-drawn sketches, Ferlinghetti adopts the role of an American bard, providing panoramic views of the Cuban Revolution in Havana, 1960, and a trip through Haiti, where Voodoo and Catholicism clash in cathedrals "filled with ulcerous children's feet running from Baron Hunger." Readers are also treated to glimpses of Ezra Pound, whom Ferlinghetti espies in Italy, as well as fellow Beat legends Allen Ginsberg and a dyspeptic William S. Burroughs, immured with his cats in a grotto-like apartment in London.

Morgan, Bill, Ed. *I Greet You at the Beginning of a Great Career: The Selected Correspondence of Lawrence Ferlinghetti and Allen Ginsberg, 1955-1997*. San Francisco: City Lights, 2015.
See entry under Allen Ginsberg.

Hettie Jones

2016

Russo, Linda. *To Think of Her Writing Awash in Light*. Boulder, CO: Subito, 2016.

> This volume features four women writers—Dorothy Wordsworth, Emily Dickinson, Hettie Jones, and Anne Waldman—and recasts their literary histories and illuminates the matter of their lives lived alongside and through poetry. Analyzing and re-imagining moments in the shift in definition over two centuries—beginning with Wordsworth's 1800

journals and ending with the completion of Waldman's epic *Iovis Trilogy* in 2012, Russo highlights the changing role of women as they emerge from the margins of literary production to take up the work of being poets. Through that lens, the essays investigate the essayist-poet's relationship to her materials, pushing at the boundaries of critical and creative writing.

Bob Kaufman

2015

Yulianto, Henrikus Joko. "Beatnik Spontaneity in the American Beat Poetry as the Image of Culture Rebels: Fostering and Transmitting a Vision of Socio-Ecological Wisdoms." *The Image of the Rebel*. Pueblo: Colorado State University, 2015. 54-64.

2014

Rice, Herbert William. "Bob Kaufman and the Limits Of Jazz." *African American Review* 47.2-3 (2014): 403-415.

Michael McClure

2015

Yulianto, Henrikus Joko. "Beatnik Spontaneity in the American Beat Poetry as the Image of Culture Rebels: Fostering and Transmitting a Vision of Socio-Ecological Wisdoms." *The Image of the Rebel*. 54-64. Pueblo: Colorado State University, 2015.

Henry Miller

2015

Calonne, David Stephen. *Henry Miller* Chicago: U Chicago P, 2015.

> In this critical biography, Calonne goes beyond Miller's notoriety to take an innovative look at the way in which the author's writings and lifestyle

were influenced by his spiritual quests. Charting Miller's cultivation of his esoteric ideas from boyhood and adolescence to later in his career, Calonne examines how Miller remained deeply engaged with a variety of philosophies, from astrology and Gnosticism to Eastern thinkers. Calonne describes not only the effects this had on Miller's work, but also on his complex and volatile life—his marriages and love affairs with Beatrice Wickens, June Mansfield, and Anaïs Nin; his years in Paris; and the journey to Greece that resulted in the travelogue *The Colossus of Maroussi*, the book Miller considered to be his greatest work. After discussing Miller's final residences in Big Sur and the Pacific Palisades in California, Calonne considers the author's involvement in the arts, love of painting and music, and friendships with a number of classical musicians. Highlighting many areas of the author's life that have previously been neglected, *Henry Miller* takes a fascinating revisionary approach to the work of one of American's most controversial and iconic writers.

Gipko, Jesse. "Road Narratives as Cultural Critiques: Henry Miller, Jack Kerouac, John Steinbeck, and William Least Heat-Moon." *Dissertation Abstracts International* 76.4 (2015).
See entry under Jack Kerouac.

Glass, Loren. "Freedom To Read: Barney Rosset, Henry Miller and the End of Obscenity." *Censorship and the Limits of the Literary: A Global View*. New York: Bloomsbury, 2015. 177-188.

Richards, Jamie Lynn. "La Vita Agra-Dolce: Italian Counter-Cultures and Translation During the Economic Miracle." *Dissertation Abstracts International* 76.2 (2015):

This dissertation focuses on Italian literature of the 1960s, specifically translations from the American counterculture and poetry of the neo-avant-garde. Through a detailed study of three specific translational moments—Fernanda Pivano's translations of Allen Ginsberg's counterculture poetry, Luciano Bianciardi's translation of Henry Miller's controversial *Tropic of Cancer*, and the neo-avant-garde poets Edoardo Sanguineti's and Alfredo Giuliani's translations of British high modernist writers such as James Joyce and T.S. Eliot—Richards explores the literary-historical period of the post-World War II economic boom in Italy. While recent translation studies scholarship focusing on Italy has addressed the Fascist period and the upsurge of translations under censorship, Richards builds upon the idea of translation as cultural resistance in order to examine the relationship between translated and original texts during a period where the explosion of industry and prosperity led intellectuals to reconsider the ideological function and purpose of art.

Sharon, Avi. "Making a New Myth Of Greece: Lawrence Durrell, Rex Warner, and the 'Captain' of Modern Greek Letters." *Arion* 23.2 (2015): 119-132.

2014

Klapaki, Nektaria G. "The Journey to Greece in the American and the Greek Modernist Literary Imagination: Henry Miller and George Seferis." *Travel, Discovery, Transformation*. New Brunswick, NJ: Transaction, 2014. 59-78.

Lambert, Josh. *Unclean Lips: Obscenity, Jews, and American Culture*. New York: New York UP, 2014.

> Jews have played an integral role in the history of obscenity in America. For most of the twentieth century, Jewish entrepreneurs and editors led the charge against obscenity laws. The anti-Semitic stereotype of the lascivious Jew has made many historians hesitant to draw a direct link between Jewishness and obscenity. In *Unclean Lips*, Josh Lambert addresses the Jewishness of participants in obscenity controversies in the U.S. directly, exploring the transformative roles played by a host of neglected figures in the development of modern and postmodern American culture. The diversity of American Jewry means that there is no single explanation for Jews' interventions in this field. Rejecting generalizations, this book offers case studies that pair cultural histories with close readings of both contested texts and trial transcripts to reveal the ways in which specific engagements with obscenity mattered to particular American Jews at discrete historical moments. Reading American culture from Theodore Dreiser and Henry Miller to *Curb Your Enthusiasm* and FCC v. Fox, *Unclean Lips* analyzes the variable historical and cultural factors that account for the central role Jews have played in the struggles over obscenity and censorship in the modern United States.

Marzoni, Andrew. "Henry Miller And Deleuze's 'Strange Anglo-American Literature'." *Understanding Deleuze, Understanding Modernism*. London: Bloomsbury, 2014. 182-195.

2013

De Bruyn, Ben. "Where to do Things with Words: Circulating Books, Decorating Rooms and Locating Modern Reading." *Orbis Litterarum* 68.6 (2013): 457-472.

> Inspired by Leah Price's recent plea on behalf of the study of "nonreading" and literary logistics, this essay reconstructs a slice of the history of reading locations by analyzing the decoration advice, the changing symbolic associations and the modes of print circulation connected with private libraries and toilets in the writings of two modern authors: Edith Wharton and Henry Miller.

Gifford, James. "From Booster to Bolero: Post-Surrealism and Apocalyptic Anarchism." *Journal of Modern Periodical Studies* 4.2 (2013): 270-298.

> This article historicizes a network of authors that coalesced around a post-surrealist aesthetic before World War II. These anarchists were destined to be overshadowed by the war, by hostile predecessors who wrote them out of history, and by progenitors who assumed the mantle of the Beats or Angry Young Men. Yet they sustained their vision from the 1940s to the 1960s, and challenged the statist politics of the high modernists and Auden Generation. Anarchism was in tune with the literary interests of the 1960s, though it proved difficult for potential allies to recognize a kindred spirit.

MacNiven, Ian S. "The Road from Delphi: Henry Miller and Greece." *Americans and the Experience of Delphi*. Boston Somerset Hall, 2013. 281-292.

Männiste, Indrek. *Henry Miller: The Inhuman Artist: A Philosophical Inquiry*. London: Bloomsbury, 2013.

> Against skeptics, Manniste argues that Miller does indeed have a philosophy of his own, which underpins most of his texts. It is demonstrated that this philosophy, as a metaphysical sense of life, forms a system the understanding of which is necessary to adequately explain even some of the most basic of Miller's ideas. Building upon his notion of the inhuman artist, Miller's philosophical foundation is revealed through his literary attacks against the metaphysical design of the modern age. It is argued that, by repudiating some of the most potent elements of late modernity such as history, modern technology and an aestheticised view of art, Miller paves

the way for overcoming Western metaphysics. Finally it is shown that, philosophically, this aim is governed by Miller's idiosyncratic concept of art, in which one is led towards self-liberation through transcending the modern society and its dehumanizing pursuits.

Masuga, Katy. "Miller's Henry and Henry's Paris." *Paris in American Literatures: On Distance as a Literary Resource*. Madison, NJ: Fairleigh Dickinson UP, 2013. 87-104.

Yang, Manuel. "Zen Buddhism as Radical Conviviality in the Works of Henry Miller, Kenneth Rexroth and Thomas Merton." *Encountering Buddhism in Twentieth-Century British and American Literature*. London: Bloomsbury, 2013. 71-87.

Charles Olson

2015

Lempert, Benjamin R. "Hughes/Olson: Whose Music? Whose Era?" *American Literature* 87.2 (2015): 303-330.

Nealand, Eireene. "Beyond The Perceptual Model: Toward A Proprioceptive Poetics." *Dissertation Abstracts International* 75.11 (2015).

In a 1965 manifesto called *Proprioception*, Charles Olson, the poet often known as the father of the American avant-garde, suggests that poets wanting to implement their open verse poetics explore a physiological faculty associated with the way we experience motion, texture, and shifts. This dissertation attempts to do so. Distinguishing between artworks associated with a perceptual model of the senses and those associated with a proprioceptive one, Nealand shows that a proprioceptive approach can be helpfully explored through a look at the work of Marcel Duchamp, who is best known for his anti-representational approach to art, one which includes the spectator as a part of the canvas. Using the example of spectator experience of a pointillist painting by Georges Seurat in which differently colored dots reach each of the viewer's eyes at different times, the dissertation shows that juxtaposition-based art allows viewers to navigate the painting using proprioceptive coordinative mechanisms to apprehend texture, seeing colors that are neither on the canvas nor in our eyes. The coordinative process, shown through a reading of the work of Jean Genet, involves not just textures associated with physical stimuli but also with memories and expectations.

Olson, Charles and Ann Charters. *Evidence of What Is Said: The Correspondence between Ann Charters and Charles Olson about History and Herman Melville.* Portland, Oregon: Tavern Books, 2015.

Evidence of What is Said is the complete correspondence between noted Beat Generation scholar and photographer Ann Charters and *The Maximus Poems* author Charles Olson. Beginning in 1968 with Charters's request for Olson to reflect on his "earliest enthusiasm for Melville," and continuing until late 1969, these letters traverse the final two years of Olson's life. Centered on Charters's book *Olson/Melville: A Study of Affinity*, the correspondence ultimately maps two writers' existence in an America that is simultaneously experiencing the wonder of the moon landing and the chaotic escalation of the Vietnam War. All the while, their exchanges navigate the convolutions of Olson's ideas about history, space, and time in relation to his pivotal book *Call Me Ishmael* and his Black Mountain College lectures. Also included in this thought-provoking epistolary is Olson's 1968 "Essay on the Matter Of," Charters's photo essay of Olson in Gloucester, and "Melville in the Berkshires," her work of experimental insight that incorporates writing by Melville.

Peters, Michael. "Sound Environment Programming the Post-1945 Moment: Charles Olson, Sun Ra, John Cage, and The Way Back In." *Dissertation Abstracts International* 76.1 (2015).

On the eve of 1945, when the Manhattan Project's machinations to split the atom were almost in place, a physicist published a little book: *What Is Life?* Applying physics to biology, Erwin Schrodinger described how genetic "code-script" could create aperiodic (non-repeating) new life from periodic materials, revealing the "secret" of life. This dilemma of life or death defines the post-1945 moment. Fraught with Hamlet-like uncertainty, this moment, as Peters argues, is the apex of a long-fomenting, eco-historical crisis where Western thinking had severed "Man" from "Nature." Sound Environment Programming is a term Peters invented to detail how Charles Olson, Sun Ra, and John Cage developed responses to this eco-historical crisis. It was a new literary science with an aperiodic means to achieve the shared aim of accessing life, a synonym for the reconnection of the human to its environment.

Rizzo, Christopher. "Critique is Not Enough: The Empirical Imperatives of Innovative American Poetry." *Dissertation Abstracts International* 76.5 (2015).

> This dissertation proposes that innovative modern and early contemporary American poetries redefine the relation of knowledge, consciousness, and poetic performance to lived experience. This study demonstrates how the radically different poetic projects of Walt Whitman, Gertrude Stein, Ezra Pound, and Charles Olson not only equally insist upon empirically investigative poetics, but also endeavor to individualize their poetic methodologies, which thus challenges the generalized Enlightenment myth of rationality. In that each of these writers undertakes to redefine the relation of knowledge, consciousness, and poetic performance to lived experience, they also undertake to rewrite our relation to the given practices of literacy that underwrite both modern and contemporary formations of culture.

Will, Frederic. *Historia: Profiles of the Historical Impulse*. Newcastle upon Tyne, UK: Cambridge Scholars, 2015.

Winslow, Aaron W. "The Labor of the Avant-Garde: Experimental Form and the Politics of Work in Post-War American Poetry and Fiction." *Dissertation Abstracts International* 76.6 (2015).
See entry under William S. Burroughs.

2014

Allison, Raphael. *Bodies on the Line: Performance and the Sixties Poetry Reading.* Iowa City: U of Iowa P, 2014.

> *Bodies on the Line* offers the first sustained study of the poetry reading in its most formative period: the 1960s. Raphael Allison closely examines a vast archive of audio recordings of several key postwar American poets to explore the social and literary context of the sixties poetry reading, which is characterized by contrasting differing styles of performance: the humanist style and the skeptical strain. The humanist style, made mainstream by the Beats and their imitators, is characterized by faith in

the power of presence, emotional communion, and affect. The skeptical strain emphasizes openness of interpretation and multivalent meaning, a lack of stability or consistency, and ironic detachment. By comparing these two dominant styles of reading, Allison argues that attention to sixties poetry readings reveals poets struggling between the kind of immediacy and presence that readings suggested and a private retreat from such performance-based publicity, one centered on the text itself. Recordings of Robert Frost, Charles Olson, Gwendolyn Brooks, Larry Eigner, and William Carlos Williams—all of whom emphasized voice, breath, and spoken language and who were inveterate professional readers in the sixties—expose this struggle in often surprising ways. In deconstructing assertions about the role and importance of the poetry reading during this period, Allison reveals just how dramatic, political, and contentious poetry readings could be.

Baptista, Cristina J. "Aura, Ambivalence, And Allure: The Portuguese in Modern American Literary Spaces." *Dissertation Abstracts International* 74.8 (2014):

This dissertation argues that modern American understandings of self and national identity emerged in relation to changing depictions of the Portuguese. Authors treated include Mark Twain, Frank Norris, Jack London, John Steinbeck, Edith Wharton, T. S. Eliot, Charles Olson, Joyce Carol Oates, and Elizabeth Bishop. While early twentieth-century American literature depicts Lusos as ignorant and swarthy figures, mid- and late twentieth-century texts dramatize the necessity of a Portuguese presence in catalyzing romantic visions of the self.

Byers, Mark. "Egocentric Predicaments: Charles Olson and the New York School of Music." *Journal of Modern Literature* 37.4 (2014): 54-69.

Grieve-Carlson, Gary. "At The Boundary Of The Mighty World: Charles Olson And Hesiod." *Mosaic* 47.4 (2014): 135-150.

Hoeynck, Joshua. "Deep Time and Process Philosophy in the Charles Olson and Robert Duncan Correspondence." *Contemporary Literature* 55.2 (2014): 336-368.

—. "Without A Mammalia Maxima, Charles Olson and Robert Duncan Apprehend a Cosmological American Poetics." *The New American Poetry: Fifty Years Later*. Bethlehem, PA: Lehigh UP, 2014. 29-58.

JBS Abstract: This essay investigates the interplay between Charles Olson and Robert Duncan. Hoeynck sees the correspondence between Olson and Duncan as producing a crucial, transformative outcome that in time most likely influenced the conceptual development of The New American Poetry.

Keelan, Claudia. "The Instant: Ecstatic Émigré 10." *American Poetry Review* 43.2 (2014): 29-30.

Middleton, Peter. "Poetry, Physics, and the Scientific Attitude at Mid-Century." *Modernism/Modernity* 21.1 (2014): 147-168.

2013

Byers, Mark. "Environmental Pedagogues: Charles Olson and R. Buckminster Fuller." *English* 62.238 (2013): 248-268.

Ford, Thomas H. "Poetry's Media." *New Literary History* 44.3 (2013): 449-469.

> Anglophone modernist poetics set out to construct poems that were things just like the other things of the world. It was a project of recapturing solidity and objectivity for poetry. In consequence, it confronted with new urgency the question of poetry's media: it was forced to clarify what the raw material of a poem actually was. Because English exists in more than one material mode—it is "verbivocovisual"—most poets understood poetry to be a mixed art, and located the poetic principle at the intersection of language's discrete material substrata. This essay examines the answers given to the question of poetry's media by Charles Olson and William Wordsworth—answers framed in both cases in atmospheric, respiratory terms. From these two cases, it sketches a media history of poetry as an aerial technology involving the transmission of breath. And it asks what implications the contemporary changing climate might have for this tradition of atmospheric poetics.

Harack, Katrina. "Representing Alterity: The Temporal Aesthetics of Susan Howe and Charles Olson." *Canadian Review of American Studies/Revue Canadienne D'etudes Americaines* 43.3 (2013): 433-461.

> Emmanuel Levinas and Elizabeth Grosz both question what it means to experience time, as well as what it means to exist with others and what it means to posit the new or unknown. These concerns are also central

to issues of American identity, and in the poetic and scholarly works of Olson and Howe, the artist is compelled to explore such an individual relationship to time even as he or she struggles to meaningfully express that relationship. They confront a tradition of American poetics and history that is framed in masculine, patriarchal terms, based on the continual tension between self and other that results in acts of colonization but also fosters innovation. This essay examines Howe's and Olson's explicit attempts to explore the nature of individual death, the experience of time and the alterity of the future, and the artistic other. They mitigate the unknown by affiliating themselves with artistic precursors (Melville and Dickinson, among others) and influence contemporary poetics, in turn.

Meyer, Andy. "'Might Be Going to Have Lived': The West in the Subjunctive Mood." *Western American Literature* 48.1-2 (2013): 201-222.

This essay works by a series of productive juxtapositions of historical, literary, and critical texts (rather than a straight linear argument) to evoke the elusive terrain of the literary West. Meyer argues that literary thinking about the West operates in the "subjunctive mood" and attempts to figure the West as a space of perpetual incompleteness. It is as grammatical a place as it is physical. From Thoreau, who stands in for a nineteenth-century imagination of the West as the potent space on which America could "write" its civic history, to Ursula K. Le Guin and her 1985 experimental utopia, *Always Coming Home*, the essay gestures toward several nineteenth- and twentieth-century writers and critics, both within and without western studies, including Adrienne Rich, Susan Howe, Charles Olson, William Carlos Williams, and earthworks artist Robert Smithson. Meyer suggests that some of the most interesting texts of the western tradition—both literary texts of the West and critical works of western studies—are informed by writers' radical self-consciousness of their own implication within the histories and power structures they simultaneously critique. Western writers must recognize their position as both products and mediators of western history.

Parent, Mikel. "Long Poems of the Short Century: Ideology and Avant-Garde Epic Form in Pound, Olson, Williams, and Zukofsky." *Dissertation Abstracts International* 74.1 (2013).

This dissertation seeks to reassess the twentieth-century epic in terms of its involvement with radical political ideologies. The study rethinks twentieth-century epic form in light of the critical work of recent decades surrounding the aftermath of Poststructuralist and Marxist approaches to theorizing modern and postmodern literature. Parent argues that the poetic form constructs ideologies rather than merely reflecting them. Specifically, Parent looks at how the avant-garde epic arose as a form of poetic construction that sought to rival the mass social movements and state forms that constructed (and continue to construct) modern and postmodern social reality. By interfacing with the historical and ideological contexts in which the poems were written, the study seeks to hold onto the importance of formal artistic processes, but without cutting off the poems from their social raw material.

Peter Orlovsky

2015

Orlovsky, Peter and Bill Morgan. *Peter Orlovsky, a Life in Words: Intimate Chronicles of a Beat Writer*. New York: Routledge, 2015.

Until now, the poet Peter Orlovsky, who was Allen Ginsberg's lover for more than 40 years, has been the neglected member of the Beat Generation. Because he lived in Ginsberg's shadow, his achievements were seldom noted and his contributions to literature have not been fully recognized. Now, this first collection of Orlovsky's writings traces his fascinating life in his own words. It also tells for the first time the intimate story of his relationship with Ginsberg. Drawn from previously unpublished journals, correspondence, photographs, and poems, the book begins as Orlovsky is discharged from the Army; follows the young man through years of self-doubt and details from his own perspective his first meeting with Ginsberg in San Francisco. In never-before-heard detail, Orlovsky describes his travels around the world with Ginsberg, Jack Kerouac, William S. Burroughs, and Gregory Corso. The book also delves into the contradictions that ultimately defined him: best known as Ginsberg's lover, Orlovsky was heterosexual and always longed to be with women; his spirit was prescient of the flower children of the sixties—especially his inclinations toward devotion and love—but in the end his use of drugs took its toll on his body and mind, silencing one of the most original and inspiring voices of his generation.

Kenneth Rexroth

Wilcke, Jonathon. "'With No Outcome in Mind': Improvisation and Improvisational Poetics in 20th-Century North American Poetry." *Dissertation Abstracts International* 75.7 (2015).
See entry for Jack Kerouac.

Gary Snyder

2014

Brown, James Patrick. "Anarchy and Individualism in American Literature: From Walden Pond to the Rise of the New Left." *Dissertation Abstracts International* 74.9 (2014).

> This dissertation tells the story of—or, rather, unfolds one intellectual history of—American individualism on the left. Brown argues that Emerson and Thoreau belong to a tradition of American anarchism that included Emma Goldman and other Gilded Age anarchists, Beat poets such as Gary Snyder and Philip Whalen, and New Leftists in the politics of the 1960s.

2013

Brown, James Patrick. "Radical Occidentalism: The Zen Anarchism of Gary Snyder and Philip Whalen." *Encountering Buddhism in Twentieth-Century British and American Literature.* London: Bloomsbury, 2013. 89-104.

Anne Waldman

2016

Russo, Linda. *To Think of Her Writing Awash in Light.* Boulder, CO: Subito, 2016.
See entry under Hettie Jones.

2014

Waldman, Anne and Laura Wright, ed. *Cross Worlds: Transcultural Poetics: An Anthology.* Minneapolis, MN: Coffee House, 2014.

Cross Worlds refers to cultural hybrids, trans-cultural alliances, and associations. This fascinating compendium documents—in essays, conversations, and Socratic raps—the vital work poets perform when they write across borders.

Lew Welch

2013

Kingston, Maxine Hong. "Lew Welch: An Appreciation." *Mānoa: A Pacific Journal Of International Writing* 25.1 (2013): 183-185.

Philip Whalen

2015

Schneider, David. *Crowded by Beauty: The Life and Zen of Poet Philip Whalen.* U of California P, 2015.
See review in this volume of the *Journal of Beat Studies*.

2014

Brown, James Patrick. "Anarchy and Individualism in American Literature: From Walden Pond to the Rise of the New Left." *Dissertation Abstracts International* 74.9 (2014).
See entry under Gary Snyder.

Call for Submissions for Volume 5: Honoring Ann Charters

The Beat Studies Association invites the submission of essays on the work and contributions to Beat Studies of the scholar Ann Charters, for the fifth volume of the *Journal of Beat Studies*, "Mapping Beat Movements 1973-present: Reading Beat Literature, Culture and Criticism Through the Works of Ann Charters."

As we, Ronna Johnson and Nancy Grace, wrote in *Breaking the Rule of Cool: Interviewing and Reading Beat Women Writers*, "Ann Charters is responsible for initiating a canon of Beat writers and writing through her prolific scholarship, criticism, and literary history focused on the Beat generation." Frankly, without her, there would be no field of Beat Studies. Charters is the founding president of the Beat Studies Association and an outstanding mentor to Beat scholars around the world.

Charters, now an emerita professor of English at The University of Connecticut at Storrs, has compiled an extremely impressive curriculum vitae, including *Bibliography of Works by Jack Kerouac* (1967); *Kerouac: A Biography* (1973); *The Beats: Literary Bohemians in Postwar America* (Dictionary of Literary Biography, 1983); *The Story and Its Writer: An Introduction to Short Fiction* (1987); *The Portable Beat Reader* (1992); the selected letters of Jack Kerouac 1940-1956 and 1957-1969 (1995, 1999); *Beat Down to Your Soul: What Was the Beat Generation?* (2001); *The Sixties* (2003); *Brother-Souls: John Clellon Holmes, Jack Kerouac, and the Beat Generation* (with Sam Charters 2010); and *Evidence of What Is Said: The Correspondence between Ann Charters and Charles Olson about History and Herman Melville* (2015). She has written on women writers of the Beat Generation and contributed many introductions to scholarly works and editions of Beat writing.

A prolific photographer, she has also published her photographs in *Blues Faces: A Portrait of the Blues* (2000); *Beats & Company: Portrait of a Literary Generation* (1986); *Olson/Melville: A Study in Affinity* (Oyez, 1968); Samuel Charters's *The Poetry of the Blues* (1963); and *Songs of Sorrow: Lucy McKim Garrison and Slave Songs of the United States* (2015). Her photo essay featuring the Nobel Prize-winning poet Tomas Tranströmer is included in Samuel Charters's translation of Tranströmer's *BALTICS* (2012).

We welcome scholarly essays on her scholarship, her work as an editor, as a photographer, and as a collaborator with her late husband Sam Charters; essays on using her anthologies in class and for research purposes; and personal testimonials from those who know her as a friend, teacher, or colleague.

Send submissions to Ronna Johnson at ronna.johnson@tufts.edu and Nancy Grace at Ngrace@wooster.edu. Deadline for submissions is July 1, 2016.

Call for Essay Proposals for an MLA Volume on Teaching Beat Generation Literature

Proposals are invited for a volume in the MLA's Options for Teaching series entitled *Teaching Beat Generation Literature*, to be edited by Nancy M. Grace. The purpose of the volume is to highlight key issues and pedagogical strategies for teaching Beat literature. The volume will include information for specialists and nonspecialists alike who are teaching at the secondary as well as undergraduate and graduate levels. A section or sections devoted to teaching resources will include teaching with images and film; teaching with anthologies; using electronic resources; and using editions, reference guides, collections of correspondence, biographies, and single author studies.

Possible topics are teaching the national and global contexts of Beat literature, major Beat writers, censorship and Beat literature, aesthetic lineages of Beat literature, Beats and the popular media, Beat fiction, Beat poetry, Beat drama, Beat film, Beat memoirs, gender and sex in Beat literature, race and ethnicity in Beat literature, Beat literature and the contemporary environmental movement, Beat writing and technology, the Beat road tale, the influence of music (jazz, in particular) on Beat writing, Beat composition philosophies and histories, drug use and Beat writing, spirituality and religious traditions in Beat writing, transhumanism and posthumanism in Beat writing, and the aesthetic and cultural legacies of Beat writing.

If you are interested in contributing an essay of 3,000 to 3,500 words, please send an abstract of 500 words in which you outline your approach or topic and how it might enhance the teaching of Beat literature to Nancy M. Grace (ngrace@wooster.edu) by July 1, 2016.

Please note that any quotations from student papers will require written permission from the students.

Essay Abstracts

William S. Burroughs, Michel Serres, and the Word Parasite
by Micheal Sean Bolton

In *Word Cultures*, Robin Lydenberg's 1987 study of William S. Burroughs's experimental novels, she devotes a chapter to the concept of the parasite as it appears in Burroughs's work. The chapter opens with a short description of Michel Serres's philosophical work *The Parasite*. She notes similarities between Serres's host/parasite binary and the binaries of the human host and the word virus and the "Other Half" in Burroughs's novels. The comparison is quite compelling, but some of the more provocative suggestions for similarities between the two writers' concepts of the host/parasite relationship are not pursued in depth. Readers are left to wonder what a more sustained examination of Serres's ideas might offer to readings of Burroughs. Cary Wolfe has recently proposed a reading of Serres's book as posthuman theory, in which the interruption of a system by parasitical noise is viewed as a necessary event in the autopoeisis of the system. This essay pursues lines of investigation suggested by Lydenberg concerning parasitical language and human subjectivity, applying such a posthuman reading to Burroughs's novels via Serres's writings on parasitical noise in order to showcase the transformative, in addition to the destructive, function of the word parasite.

The Beats and Independent Film: A Different Cast of Characters
by Jane Falk

This essay presents both an expanded yet more focused view of independent Beat film with a slightly different cast of characters: Beat women. As actors, women were given somewhat objectified roles, while as filmmakers themselves, they provided roles in which women were empowered and at times dominant. Writers discussed in the essay are Diane di Prima, Lenore Kandel, ruth weiss, Helen Adam, and Joanne Kyger.

Allen Ginsbserg's Ambivalent Whitman
by Anne Lovering Rounds

In his poems of New York, most notably in "Crossing Brooklyn Ferry," Whitman articulates a fundamental tension: while the city is continuously connective, urban growth and encounter necessarily encompass the death of the city poet. This essay sketches the ways Allen Ginsberg, who gestures to Whitman throughout his career, articulates and continues this dynamic in his own poetry of New York. As it considers Ginsberg's inheritance of an urban pastoral sensibility from Whitman, the essay catalogs different ways death, decay, and mortality figure into Ginsberg's New York.

Gary Snyder, Counterculture, and National Identity
by John Whalen-Bridge

This essay explores the development of Gary Snyder's countercultural thought in relation to the way he refers to "the United States of America." In the early and middle parts of his career, it is as if America is the national that shall not be named, and he displaces reference to it, calling it "Turtle Island," or he refers to bioregional identity as trumping national identity or political boundaries in terms of long term. Is he "radical" or "avant-garde"? Snyder has famously claimed to be the poet who holds the oldest possible values, placing himself within a Paleolithic world-view. *His* army does not directly engage with such enemies as the neo-liberal state, unquestioned urban ideology that relegates wilderness to the status of recreational entertainment, or the quadrennial battles to install a symbol in the White House. As his poetry illustrates, he would rather have us think in terms of centuries or chunks of time on the order of 50,000 years. In a way that harkens back to Robinson Jeffers's "inhumanism," Snyder nudges readers beyond the humanist scale of time that focuses on the next 20 or 50 years, a period that will directly affect us and our children.

Notes on Contributors

Micheal Sean Bolton teaches at the American University in Dubai. His field of research is in United States experimental fiction of the 20th century. He is the author of *Mosaic of Juxtaposition: William S. Burroughs' Narrative Revolution* (Rodopi, 2014), a study of William S. Burroughs's experimental novels. His publications also include articles in *The Flannery O'Connor Review, JNT: Journal of Narrative Theory*, and the essay collection *The Beats and Philosophy*. He has published poetry in journals including *Prism International, Mad Hatters' Review*, and *Otoliths*.

Maria Damon is professor and chair of Humanities and Media Studies at the Pratt Institute of Art. She is the author of *Postliterary America: From Bagel Shop Jazz to Micropoetries* (North American Poetry, 2011), *Dark End of the Street: Margins in American Vanguard Poetry* (U of Minnesota P, 1993); co-editor with Ira Livingston of *Poetry and Cultural Studies: A Reader* (U of Illinois P, 1999), co-author of several books of poetry and book-length online poems, and of two books of cross-stitch visual poetry.

Michael Dittman is an assistant professor of English at Butler County Community College. He is the author of *Jack Kerouac: A Biography* (Greenwood, 2004).

Jane Falk is retired from the University of Akron, where she served as a senior lecturer. Her research and scholarship focuses on Joanne Kyger, Philip Whalen, Zen Buddhism and the Beats, and Beats and independent film. Her essay on Joanne Kyger and philosophy appeared in the essay collection *The Beats and Philosophy*.

Amy Friedman is an assistant professor of English at Temple University. She teaches courses on satire, Anglo-American women modernists, composition with a focus on environmental justice, and the Beat Generation. Friedman has a chapter about the work of Rochelle Owens in the forthcoming book *Beat Drama: Playwrights and Performances of the "Howl" Generation*, edited by Deborah Geis (Methuen Press).

Todd Giles is an assistant professor of English at Midwestern State University in Wichita Falls, Texas, where he teaches a wide range of undergraduate and graduate courses, including postmodern American literature, ecocriticism, and Zen and the Beats. His scholarship, which appears in journals such as *Philosophy and Literature, Texas Studies in Language and Literature, Popular Culture Review*, and *Journal of Beat Studies*, focuses on the cross-fertilization of American literature, music, philosophy, and the visual arts. He is associate editor/book review editor of the *William Carlos Williams Review*.

NOTES ON CONTRIBUTORS

Anne Lovering Rounds is a poet and assistant professor of English at Hostos Community College, a campus of the City University of New York located in the South Bronx. Her creative and critical work has appeared in journals including *Hartskill Review, Literary Imagination, New Writing, Penny Ante Feud, Proteus,* and *Text Matters*. Her first poetry collection, *Variations in an Emergency*, is the recipient of the 2014 Cathlamet Prize from Ravenna Press and is forthcoming in 2017.

Jack Ryan is vice provost, dean of arts and humanities, and associate professor of English at Gettysburg College. He is the author of *John Sayles, Filmmaker* (McFarland, 2010). He has also published articles in *Isle: Interdisciplinary Studies in Literature and the Environment, Creative Screenwriting,* and *Aethlon: The Journal of Sport and Literature*.

Jennie Skerl is a founding board member and past president of the Beat Studies Association. She has published *William S. Burroughs* (Twayne, 1985), *William S. Burroughs at the Front: Critical Reception, 1959-1989* (co-edited with Robin Lydenberg, Southern Illinois U P, 1991), *A Tawdry Place of Salvation: The Art of Jane Bowles* (Southern Illinois UP, 1997), *Reconstructing the Beats* (Palgrave Macmillan, 2004), and *The Transnational Beat Generation,* (co-edited with Nancy M. Grace, Palgrave Macmillan, 2012). Skerl has published invited introductions to the 25th anniversary edition of *Naked Lunch* (Grove, 1984), *Speed* by William Burroughs, Jr. (Overlook, 1984), *William S. Burroughs: Time-Place-Word* (Brown University exhibit catalog, ed. Eric Shoaf, 2000), and the foreword to *Retaking the Universe: William Burroughs in the Age of Globalization* (ed. Davis Shneiderman and Philip Walsh, Pluto, 2004).

Katharine Streip is an associate professor in the Liberal Arts College at Concordia University, Montreal, Quebec. She has published articles on Jean Rhys, Marcel Proust, Philip Roth, William S. Burroughs, James Joyce, Franz Kafka, and zombies. Her research interests include media theory, new materialisms, subjectivity, comedy, the novel, affect theory, popular culture, ecocriticism, and avant-garde movements. She is writing a book on media and subjectivity and a monograph on William S. Burroughs.

John Whalen-Bridge is associate professor of English at the National University of Singapore. Author of *Political Fiction and the American Self* (1998), he has co-edited (with Gary Storhoff) the SUNY series "Buddhism and American Culture." This series includes *The Emergence of Buddhist American Literature* (2009), *American Buddhism as a Way of Life* (2010), *Writing as Enlightenment* (2010), and *Buddhism and American Cinema* (2015). "What is a Buddhist Movie?"

(*Contemporary Buddhism*) and "Multiple Modernities and the Tibetan Diaspora" (*South Asian Diaspora*) explore Tibetan expression and representation, and *Tibet on Fire: Buddhism, Rhetoric, and Self-Immolation* (Palgrave, 2015) approaches Tibetan responses to censorship through the lens of Kenneth Burke's notion of dramatism.

Editorial Policy

The *Journal of Beat Studies* invites articles on the works of Beat movement writers and their colleagues, especially New York School, Black Mountain School, and San Francisco Renaissance writers, as well as those connected to these movements, in the United States and globally. The *Journal* intends to represent the breadth and eclecticism of critical approaches to Beat Generation writers, and welcomes new perspectives and contexts of inquiry.

Articles that are deemed appropriate are sent for review anonymously to a member of the Editorial Board and at least one other reader. Manuscripts should not be under consideration elsewhere, and we do not publish previously published work. It is strongly advised that those submitting work to *JBS* be familiar with the journal's content. Among criteria on which evaluation of submissions depends are whether an article demonstrates recognition of and thorough familiarity with scholarship already published in the field, whether the article is written clearly and effectively, and whether it makes a genuine contribution to Beat studies.

Preparation of Copy

1. Articles are typically between 25 and 30 pages, and do not exceed 9000 words, including notes and works cited. Inquiries about significantly shorter or longer submissions should be sent to the editors.

2. A separate page should include the article's title, author's name, address, telephone & fax numbers, and e-mail address. The author's name and identifying references should not appear on the manuscript to preserve anonymity for our readers.

3. All submissions must include an abstract of no more than 250 words.

4. The manuscript should be in Times New Roman 12, double-spaced, and should adhere to the most recent MLA style.

5. Submissions may be sent by email as word documents ("doc" only, not "docx") to Ronna C. Johnson (ronna.johnson@tufts.edu) and Nancy M. Grace (ngrace@wooster.edu) simultaneously. Mailed submissions may be sent to Nancy M. Grace, Department of English, 400 E. University Street, The College of Wooster, Wooster, Ohio 44691. For mailed submissions, please send three copies of the article and abstract.

6. Submissions may also be sent via the online submission form at http://www.beatstudies.org/jbs/submission_guidelines.html.

7. Authors of accepted manuscripts are responsible for any necessary permissions fees and for securing any necessary permissions.

8. All editorial, review, and advertising inquiries should be addressed to ronna.johnson@tufts.edu and ngrace@wooster.edu.

9. Inquiries concerning orders should be addressed to PaceUP@pace.edu.

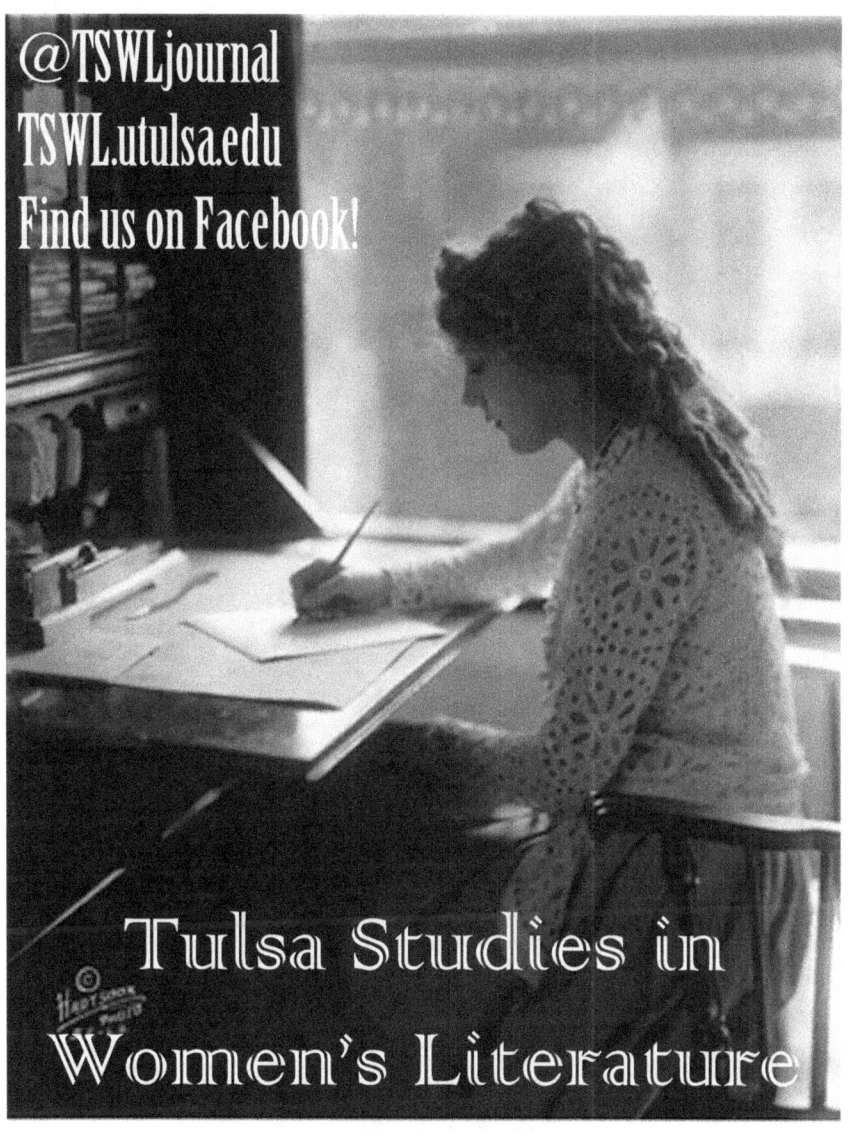

The fourth volume of *Journal of Beat Studies*
was published in Spring 2016
by Pace University Press

Cover and Interior Design by Mary Katherine Cornfield
The journal was typeset in Times New Roman and AmerType Md BT
and printed by Lightning Source in La Vergne, Tennessee

Pace University Press

Director: Sherman Raskin
Associate Director: Manuela Soares
Marketing Manager: Patricia Hinds
Design Consultant: Sara Yager
Production Editor: Stephanie Hsu

Graduate Assistants: Mary Katherine Cornfield and Angela Taldone
Student Aide: Kelsey O'Brien-Enders

www.ingramcontent.com/pod-product-compliance
Lightning Source LLC
Chambersburg PA
CBHW061450300426
44114CB00014B/1921